THE $5 LUNCH
New York City

50 Exceptional Places
for $5 or Less

TIMES SQUARE AREA

Jeffrey Shubart
and Eddie Sugarman

SUGARSHU BOOKS • NEW YORK CITY, NEW YORK

The authors have not received or accepted free food, money or
any other remuneration from an employee, owner or homeless
guy associated with any of the establishments mentioned in
this guide. At the time of this guide's printing, all information
contained herein was accurate to the best of our knowledge;
however, due to the volatility of the economy and the restaurant industry, prices may change and restaurants may close or
move. While writing this guide, Jeffrey's cholesterol count
soared from 120 to 400 (and counting). Eddie can no longer fit
into his jeans and is easily winded when walking uphill.

"Ask not what you can do
for your country. Ask
what's for lunch."

ORSON WELLES

Dedication

For Joanna and Kara. We love you.

And for Sam. If this sells 50,000 copies,
you can go to private school.

Thanks!

Greg Forgach, for your amazing creativity and input in the design process.

Howard Freeman, for nailing all those cover design deadlines between meals at the Vegas buffets.

John Halmi, for your company and encouragement as you tagged along for free food.

Dina Kalman, for your time, talent and greed for sushi.

Maida Landau-Bruck, for your invaluable help with the book's layout.

Maureen Mankowitz, for your raspy voice and for never questioning our time sheets.

Jeff Marx, the author of *How To Win A High School Election*, for generously sharing your first-hand knowledge of the self-publishing world.

David Saylor, of Scholastic Books, for checking out our cover design.

And all our friends and family, our extra sets of eyes, who helped bring this book to fruition.

Table of contents

Intro

We are very proud to provide you with this guide to the 50 best places in the Times Square area to eat lunch for $5 or less, including tax and tip. New York is an expensive city, Manhattan is its most expensive borough and Times Square is like some nightmarish money vacuum that never needs to have its bag changed and has way too many revivals playing. That's why lunching for less feels so good. Staying at $5 or less is awesome; it means you've beaten Times Square at its own overpriced game and you've got the bills in your pocket to prove it.

In addition to having great prices, each of these eateries is fantastic in its own way. Taste, of course, was the most important factor in our decision to include a restaurant in this guide. However, cuisine, portion size, cleanliness and unique-New-York-ness were important considerations as well.

• If you are one of the 26 million tourists that visit Times Square annually, save a couple dollars, yen or euros on your lunch tab. Spend the big bills on dinner at The 21 Club and orchestra tickets to a Broadway show; don't blow your budget on lunch!

• If you are one of the 2.5 million employees working in the area, we feel your pain! How many more times can you order delivery from that same old Chinese place before you jam a chopstick into your eye to relieve the monotony? You now hold in your hand 50 less invasive alternatives.

• If you are one of the 27,000 Times Square residents...you've got to eat, right? Besides, that tiny little kitchen of yours is a pain in the butt to clean and your ancient oven heats up the whole apartment and keeps setting off the fire alarm.

So if you find yourself in Times Square for a day or a lifetime, turn the page and join us in the revolt against high-priced lunches.

Chow!

Jeffrey Shubart & Eddie Sugarman

For the purposes of this guide, the Times Square area stretches from Port Authority (40th Street) on the south to Central Park (59th Street) on the north and from Ninth Avenue on the west to Fifth Avenue on the East.

Map Key / Restaurant Listing

Denotes a street-cart that may migrate. Location on map is its usual location at time of printing.

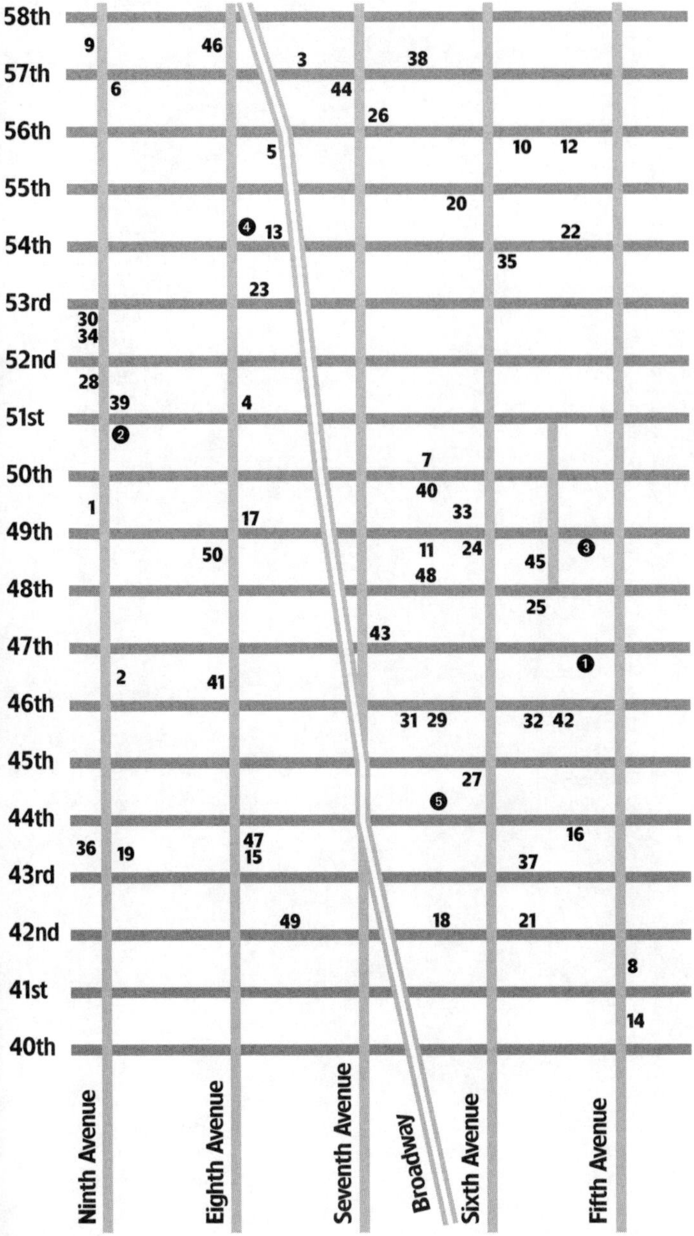
58th
57th
56th
55th
54th
53rd
52nd
51st
50th
49th
48th
47th
46th
45th
44th
43rd
42nd
41st
40th
Ninth Avenue
Eighth Avenue
Seventh Avenue
Broadway
Sixth Avenue
Fifth Avenue
9 46 3 38
6 44 26
5 10 12
20
4 13 22
35
23
30
34
28
39 4
2
7
40
1 17 33
50 11 24 45 3
48
25
43
1
2 41
31 29 32 42
27
5
36 19 47 15 16
37
49 18 21
8
14

Amish Market

Market/Grocery

731 Ninth Ave. (bet. 49th and 50th streets)
Seven days, 7 a.m. – 9:30 p.m.
(212) 245-2360

Harrison Ford would have gained 20 pounds if they had filmed *Witness* at the Amish Market, a gourmet grocery store where you could easily drop a wad of cash on fancy imported foods and mouth-watering baked goods. Among their forest of high prices, however, are tag-sale priced morsels that can make up a wonderful three-course lunch.

Appetizer: Free samples abound. Who knows what you'll get? Sliced honey-soaked apricots? Bits of tantalizing imported cheeses? Round out your first course with the back corner olive oasis. Like a boutique olive shop on the Riviera, Amish Market offers free samples of more than twenty varieties. No pimentos here, folks. High-end olives such as the Assaigo Classico and the deep purple Chilean Alphonso are invitingly displayed in over-sized rustic wooden bowls. And if the freebies hook you, happily bag them up for $4.89 a pound.

Main course: Very generous helpings of cold soups are available, $3.49 for a large or $2.98 for a small. The gazpacho is excruciatingly good; chock full of basil, it's more flavorful than it is five-alarm spicy. Also featured are a very nice cucumber soup, an unusual but tasty mango soup and many others such as asparagus and carrot dill. Deli salads come pre-packaged in half-pound containers. Since the seafood and chicken salads price out the same per pound, go for the better of the two: the sensational chicken. Mixed with creamy Dijon mayonnaise, it is sprinkled with tiny celery flecks for optimal crunchiness. A half-pound container will cost you approximately $3.50. They also turn out pricey pre-packaged gourmet sandwiches, which go half price after 6 p.m. You can irritate Dr. Atkins by complementing your meal with one of eight varieties of rolls at the bakery. Starchy dunkers like the Portuguese hero or a mini ciabatta range from 50¢ to 69¢.

Dessert: Fruit for dessert? Your mom would be so proud! Take your pick from some of the sweetest and most varied produce in midtown, like a juicy kiwi for a quarter or a bag of plump Washington cherries for 50¢.

Since there's no seating in the Amish Market, ask for utensils and enjoy your lunch down the block at the World Wide Plaza.

Amy's Bread

Bakery, Sandwiches

672 Ninth Ave. (bet. 46th and 47th streets)
Monday – Friday, 7:30 a.m. – 11 p.m.
Saturday, 8 a.m. – 11 p.m.
Sunday, 9 a.m. – 6 p.m.
(212) 977-2670
www.amysbread.com

Rising to the occasion for very little dough, Amy's Bread, with its charming afternoon-tea décor, attracts a bevy of regulars devoted to Amy's divine loaves of freshly baked bread. Amy's Bread is, however, much more than just a bakery churning out the best bread in Hell's Kitchen. With an impressive selection of high-end sandwiches served on delicious bread, and a fantastic variety of baked goods, Amy's Bread is the place to go for a taste of serenity in the heart of the city.

As you enter past the beautiful window display of freshly baked bread, grab a spot at one of the six small tables. And make sure you're sitting down when you bite into what is unquestionably our favorite of all the wonderful sandwiches – roast turkey on semolina raisin and fennel bread with cranberry sauce – 'cause it'll knock you off your feet when you taste Thanksgiving between two slices of heaven. The dollop of cranberry sauce combined with fresh turkey and the raisins in the delicious bread, makes this the Thanksgiving left-over sandwich of our dreams.

You could also go for a mini-sandwich, and add one of a plethora of fantastic baked goods. How's this for a combination? A mozzarella and tomato mini served with the lightest drizzle of oil and balsamic vinegar on a thick dowel of fragrant olive fennel bread accompanied by freshly baked Irish soda bread. Or substitute a scone, cookie, bread twist, roll, muffin or some other snack. Our recommendation? The applesauce doughnut: moist orchard-sweet dough with a pleasingly firm cinnamon-flecked crust.

The atmosphere of the tiny dining area is delightful. There are magazines for your perusal, and a view of the bakery machinery through the transparent back wall. At 6 p.m., Amy's Bread adds its late night menu, which includes a toasted Brie and apple sandwich for a mere $3.75. You might have to think about coming back for dinner.

Associated Supermarket / Morton Williams Cafe

Supermarket

225 W. 57th St. (bet. Broadway & Seventh Ave.)
(212) 581-7200
Monday – Sunday, 11 a.m. – 1 a.m.

Sam's Club may have thirty pound boxes of Cheerios for wholesale, but Associated Supermarkets has a variety of beautiful seating options at which to enjoy its fantastic selection of less than $5 lunches.

At the pizza counter, a tempting sign boasts "individual pizza with sausage, pepperoni & peppers - $1.75". Skip this poor cousin to Stouffer's toaster pizza, however. Upgrade instead to the $3.99 small round pie which is tasty and more than sufficient for two (toppings .50¢ per). They also hawk a sausage, cheese and roasted pepper roll ($2.95) and Parmigiana sandwiches (chicken, meatball, eggplant or sausage) for $4.50.

Over yonder at the grill, the best deal is a turkey, veggie or beef burger deluxe with lettuce, tomato and steak fries ($4.50). It's grilled then-and-there and the whole package is a good gut-full. At the grill, you can also snag a half roasted chicken ($3.95) or an enormous overstuffed baked potato ($2.95).

If one of the two-seat tables on the window is free, grab it for people watching. Otherwise, descend to the attractive and spacious downstairs. Colorful images of balloons superimposed on the city's skyline surround the area and you can check out the kitchen through a Plexiglas viewing panel. Best of all, there's a microwave that increases your options by leaps and bounds. Upstairs next to the salad bar and near two huge disembodied toy dinosaur heads (seriously!) is a display of prepared foods for heating and eating. The many selections, depending on which day you stroll in, might include mushroom knishes ($1.39), beef quesadillas ($4.49) and macaroni and cheese ($2.27). On the colder side is German potato salad ($2.19), a very generous container of fruit salad ($2.50), or – at the sushi bar - you can lay $4.25 down for a California roll, or $4.50 for a spicy salmon roll.

Advantages to grocery store eating include skipping ATM fees by paying with your debit card and getting cash back. Heck, do some shopping while you're here and save yourself oodles of time. Special bonus! Bored cashiers mean careless discounts from time to time.

Bagel Café

Bakery, Sandwiches

850 Eighth Ave. (NE corner of 51st Street)
Seven days, 5 a.m. – 1 a.m.
(212) 262-7437

Everything at the Bagel Café, as expected, is centered around the bagels. The usual bagel suspects crowd the counter glass along side cookies, Danishes and muffins, vying for your attention. And your eye could easily settle on one of the gigantic muffins, particularly their amazing apple muffin ($2). Closer to a muffin-shaped apple coffeecake, this apple bomb (whose sheer weight in butter is compelling) and a cup of coffee almost make a meal alone.

But the real deal here is one of their deli sandwiches on a warm sliced bagel (ask which bagels are still hot for the ultimate in sandwich bagelry). For $4.50 – $4.65, you can get turkey, salami, mozzarella and tomato, salmon salad or tuna salad on a bagel. Our choice is the tuna. For one thing, there's a lot of it. For another, they sagaciously mix in finely chopped celery for a nice little crunch. Most importantly, let's talk about mayo. Our moms must be moonlighting at Bagel Deli, because the tuna salad has the perfect mom-amount of mayo. You know, just shy of the amount that would cause your heart to burst. Finally, a word about tuna salad on a bagel in general; it's the only way to go! The tuna is squishy enough that a nice dollop of it rises up through the bagel hole as if to say, "Hello, would you like to eat me?" Don't mind if we do.

How about 10 varieties of omelets? Many of them
are $3.50 such as the Mexican, Spanish with cel-
ery, cheese, broccoli and mushroom. Sit down
now, because for a mere $4.50 you can get the
grand-daddy of New York breakfasts: a lox omelet.
What a price! And each one comes with a fresh
bagel of your choice.

Bagel Café is much more comfortable than it looks
from the outside. Their big weathered mirrors
reflect the café's pleasant view. The staff is relaxed
and polite and there is a variety of seating choices.
Roomy counters line the 51st Street window for
people watching, a section of tables beckons tradi-
tionalists and a few scattered high tables with
those narrow wobbly chairs dare you to sit in them
successfully.

Balsley Café

Sandwiches, Soup/Salad

SE corner of 57th Street and Ninth Avenue
Seven days, 7 a.m. – 4 p.m.
(212) 489-1194

Until recently, the southeast corner of 57th Street
and Ninth Avenue was a blemish on the face of
midtown. Then the city intervened and built
Balsley Park, a very small yet pretty park flush with
ferns and shade. And soon thereafter came Balsley
Café, a kiosk with a small menu as refreshing as
the park itself. Now, the formerly blighted corner is
a home to sunbathers and tourists looking for a
respite from the overpriced theme restaurants on
57th Street.

Balsley Café offers seven small wraps for $3 or
less, which, when combined with your choice of
two 75¢ sides like chips and cole slaw, make a
nice picnic lunch. If you go the wrap route, sink
your teeth into the grilled chicken Caesar. The
chicken is fresh and lightly peppered, a hearty
complement to the zesty Caesar dressing. And you
fish haters can breathe a sigh of relief; this thick
dressing (on the side) contains very little anchovy
paste. Although many of the wraps are pre-made,
the lettuce and tomato stay crisp and cool.

Balsley Café also serves soup and salad, although
the salad platters are not served on weekends. But
if you happen to stop by when the soup of the day
is chicken noodle, you're in for a treat. The broth

is thick and satisfying and the chicken is real (can I get a witness!), not that fake processed meat you find in most corner deli soups. Overall, the soup is salt-a-licious and you'd be hard pressed to find a better chicken noodle in midtown from a place not named The Soup Nazi.

Of course, one of the delights of eating at the Balsley Café is the park itself. You can eat at one of the dozen or so post-modern, industrial silver tables, or go picnic on the small grassy knoll, where no conspiracy theories are brewing (that we know of). And if you happen by on a Saturday during the spring to Christmas season, you can pick up some groceries at the Farmers Market that runs down Ninth Avenue between 57th and 56th streets.

Baluchi's

Indian

240 W. 56th St. (bet. Broadway and Eighth Ave.)
Seven days, 12 p.m. – 10:30 p.m.
(212) 397-0707
www.baluchis.com

Baluchi's sounds Italian, but is actually an Indian restaurant that boasts one of the greatest lunch specials in Manhattan. Their entire menu of Indian delicacies is 50% off every day from noon until 3 p.m. (dine-in only).

Although their entrées are pricey ($11.95 and up), Baluchi's appetizers are inexpensive, scrumptious and filling. With fourteen choices coming out of the Tandoor for less than $5 (with discount), it's a good thing the menu is tourist friendly, precisely describing each dish for the uninitiated.

The chicken tikka starter ($7.95 before discount) is succulent and well presented. Marinated in ginger, garlic and yogurt, three boneless pieces of tikka are served on a bed of lettuce and garnished with tomato and lemon. Another dish, ka-chori, is accurately described in the menu as "too difficult to put into words but recommended." What the hell, though; we'll try. Ka-chori is a blend of different chutneys, chilies and chickpeas (say that 10 times fast!) atop a lentil patty. Don't let unfamiliarity scare you off or you'll miss this beautiful combination of flavors: delicious and sweet with a mashed potato consistency. Upon request you get a complimentary plate of mango chutney, pickles, red onions and green chilies, all of which go well with just about everything. A basket of paddad, a thin crunchy wafer-like bread, comes with the condiments as well.

For those who want to spend a little more, they offer a tempting $12.95 special ($6.50 with the discount) that includes an appetizer, entrée, basmatti rice, nan bread, cucumber, raita (yogurt) and mango chutney.

The décor is fantastic, with large copper goblets topping wildly designed tables. Percussive Indian music permeates the restaurant and the service is pleasant and quick.

The Border A La Carta

Mexican, Street-cart

South side of 50th Street (west of Sixth Avenue)
Monday – Friday, 11:30 a.m. – 3:30 p.m.

The Border A La Carta is the only Mexican street-cart we've come across in our manifold travels of the Times Square area. The ingredients here are all fresh and piping hot or crisply cold as appropriate. So when that commercial whines "run for the border", do as it says and come to this sparkling clean break from street-cart monotony.

The burrito platter is prodigious and weighty. You get a chicken or beef burrito stuffed with goodies and then geometrically jammed into one side of a square Styrofoam container. The other half of the container is crammed with rice and creamy refried beans and topped with melted nacho cheese. The burrito itself is packed with juicy shredded chicken, lettuce, tomato, sour cream and (if you dare) hot hot hot jalapeños. The rice and beans are tasty and filling, but beware; the later it gets in the day, the more likely you are to get your beans scorched.

The platters are also the best deal dollars and cents wise. Rice and beans alone costs $3. Add rice and beans to a taco to make a taco platter and your price jumps from $2.50 to $4. The burrito platter ($5), however, is only $1 more than a plain burrito ($4). You with us?

If you're in a crunchy mood, go for the taco. Nope,

(continued)

it's not a soft taco. Doesn't anyone serve an old-fashioned crispy messy ground-beef-all-over-my-slacks taco anymore? The Border A La Carta does, thank you very much.

Cue up early, it's a trendy spot. As with most of the street-carts we've included in this guide, the owner/operators of this stand are incredibly friendly and helpful. Treat the el fuego with care, but don't sweat it too much, they have plenty of cold drinks to assuage any hot sauce victims.

"New York is the greatest city in the world for lunch."

WILLIAM EMERSON, JR.

Bread Market Café

Baked Potatoes, Soup/Salad

485 Fifth Ave. (bet. 41st and 42nd streets)
Monday – Saturday, 6 a.m. – 5 p.m.
(212) 370-7356

Bread Market Café is an up-scale deli catering to the business elite who have little time and high expectations. No tables here, just a few stools at a shimmering silver countertop with a 50 yard-line view of the New York Public Library.

At the impressive baked potato bar, you can behave with a steamed vegetable potato or pig out on a bacon and cheddar spud for ($4.50). It's one of the very few places to use real strips of crispy bacon. The Potato King himself only uses Bacon Bits!

Bread Market offers a very trendy salad bar where your greens are mixed and matched to your liking. The small starts at $2.50, the medium at $3.50 and the large at $3.95. Added ingredients, aside from the free croutons and onions, begin at 50¢. Marinated tofu is one of the many alluring items with which you can spiff up your spinach, romaine or mesclun.

During normal lunch hours, they get crazy busy. So go early or late or be prepared to wait. You can reward yourself when you get to the counter by giving the person behind you an aneurysm by calmly and slowly asking for free samples of each of their seven tasty daily soups. We highly recommend the salty but delicious Italian wedding soup with its little bits of pasta and spinach in each bite. The cream of asparagus is good too: hearty, not heavy. Individual quiches and fresh berry and yogurt parfaits are options for $3.95.

"A man may be a pessimistic determinist before lunch and an optimistic believer in the will's freedom after it."

ALDOUS HUXLEY

Burrito Box

Mexican

885 Ninth Ave. (bet. 57th and 58th streets)
Seven days, 11 a.m. – 11:30 p.m.
(212) 489-6889

We were all shocked recently when longtime cheap favorite Burrito World was bought out by the not-so-cheap Lunch Box across the street and assimilated into Burrito Box. Change is scary, but c'mon, we've all read *Who Moved My Cheese?* and know that new cheese can be better than old cheese.

Burrito Box grills up generous 12" stuffed flour quesadillas, which are folded and sliced into gooey strips. You can nab three of their 11 varieties for less than a Lincoln, the best being the mixed vegetable quesadilla ($4.25). It's stuffed with zucchini, carrots, corn and green peppers and is served with guacamole, sour cream and pico de gallo. Some kind of yummy melted cheese holds the whole operation together like a delicious dairy crazy-glue.

There are nine different kinds of cheap taco selections, and two tacos come to an order. Decisions, decisions: will you get the chicken ranchero, BBQ chicken, chili con carne, spinach, guacamole or rice and beans? Hard shell or soft?! Well, if you ask real nice, they'll let you indecisive Libras mix and match. You can get, for example, a guacamole hard shell and a chicken ranchero soft shell taco for $4.55. Free pico de gallo, guacamole, sour

31

cream and lettuce to boot.

The atmosphere, if predictably Tex-Mex, is delight-fully bright and clean. Burrito Box features a spread of free chips and salsa and water on the counter to make the wait more pleasant. Upon request you can substitute brown rice (perfect with their spinach selections), tofu sour cream, pinto beans or whole-wheat tortillas in any of the selections.

"What contemptible scoundrel
has stolen the cork to
my lunch?"

W.C. FIELDS

Cucina Gourmet

Pizza

54 W. 56th St. (bet. Fifth and Sixth avenues)
Monday – Friday, 7 a.m. – 5 p.m.
(212) 262-0909

Cucina Gourmet recently acquired the storefront next door and has expanded their pizza repertoire to slices, calzones, chicken rolls and other pizza-counter fare. Cucina still specializes, however, in pizzettes, which are basically individual Boboli's. Remember Bobolis from the grocery store; you buy a hearty pre-made crust and pile on toppings, cheese and sauce and pop it in the oven? Well at Cucina's, you get any topping you want and Boboli-style focaccia-thick dough, but they do all the work. It's made to order, so expect to wait about eight minutes.

A small is just $3, a large will run you $4, and toppings are 50¢ apiece. The fun and fancy items to pick from include: marinated roasted red peppers, grilled diced eggplant, jalapeño cheese, roasted tomato, fresh basil and diced sun-dried tomatoes. In fact, they'll put anything they have from their well-stocked salad bar on your pizzette. You want tabouli pizza? You got it. How about a hummus and couscous 'za? Disgusting, but they'll do it.

A pepperoni-topped pizzette is a great choice. Their distinctive pepperoni slices are not the communion wafer sized ones we're all used to. One humongous slice of the pepperoni covers the entire toppings area of the pizzette, which, by the way, is about seven inches in diameter and served in quarters. The crust is flavorful and solid enough to defy the dreaded pizza droop syndrome. The cheese is gooey and hot, but not the napalm magma you sometimes get that destroys your taste buds for a week.

It's possible you might be stuffed before setting one foot in the place. There is often a staff member at the front door beckoning and bribing passersby with free samples of bruschetta like an Italian carnival barker. The bruschetta is unusual and light – carrots and cucumbers in a light dill pesto sauce atop a small piece of crisp French bread.

The recent demise of Rosella Pizza makes Cucina the pizza champ of its stretch of 56th Street. Watch your back though, Cucina. This here's a tough pizza town.

Cynthia & Robert

Hot Dogs/Sausages, Street-cart
South side of 49th Street (west of Sixth Avenue)
Monday – Friday, 11 a.m. – 5 p.m.

This fine street-cart establishment opened in 1975 and 27 years later they're still doing strong business. Cynthia & Robert's staying power can be attributed to great service and preposterously delicious sausages.

Smokey and savory, a Cynthia & Robert sausage is the cornerstone of a fine and filling cheap sandwich ($4.25). Unlike many street-cart vendors, Cynthia and Robert take their time preparing their wares. The sausage sandwich, their best seller, spotlights the sausage, which is split and laid flat. The tangy special sauce they add does not over-power, but compliments the sausage's rich flavors, and diced peppers and onions contribute crunchy texture as well as flavor to the overall package.

According to the owners, the Philly cheesesteak is their second most popular item. They also serve hoagies filled with hot turkey ($3.75), pastrami ($4.25) and chicken or eggplant Parmigiana ($4.25). C&R fry up a very nice shrimp hoagie too ($4.25) stuffed with green pepper, onion, lettuce, tomato and a delicious garlic sauce you can smell from ten blocks away.

Aesthetically, this street-cart is certainly one of the most interesting we've seen. An enormous plate of sausages stacked precariously high adorns the front window, old laminated reviews are pasted on the west side of the cart and a weatherworn sign rises from the top of the cart proudly proclaiming over 25 years of existence. On one side, they've built a transparent insulated box that holds dozens of seeded hoagie rolls. Cynthia and Robert have built quite a cozy little nest for themselves that they squeeze into every day to serve the huge lines of hungry folk jonesin' for some sausage.

"Reservations and cloth napkins are really minor pinnacles in the high sierra of the New York lunch."

RAYMOND SOKOLOV

D&S Marketplace

Burgers, Sandwiches

**34 W. 56th Street (bet. Fifth and Sixth avenues)
Monday – Saturday, 7 a.m. – 7 p.m.
(212) 265-3434**

You'd think that Britney Spears was autographing cans of Pepsi here the way the line literally goes out the door during the lunch rush. Nope. It's simply good food for great prices that makes D&S a regular spot for area cubicle-jockeys.

Big, easy-to-read signs point out the daily sandwich specials at the deli-counter. Favorites like chicken Parmigiana ($4.50), BBQ grilled chicken ($4.50) and tuna ($4) are turned out at blinding speed, but still the mammoth line remains. What's a staffer on a deadline or a tourist with a matinee to catch to do? The solution is the express grill line. If you're pressed for time, go to the front of the class where the wait is just a minute or two for grilled yummies like a Philly cheesesteak or a burger. Cheeseburgers, veggie burgers and turkey burgers come deluxe (lettuce, tomato and French fries) for only $4.50. It's a tasty good-sized burger that gets big points for its toasted bun and an entire pickle on the side; that's above and beyond as far as cheap burgers go. The fries are fresh and hot: gleaming with tasty coronary horror.

For $4.50, they sell a wonderful vegetarian sandwich that can only be described as beefy. You could shot-put this sucker a good stretch. Julienne carrots, lettuce, muenster cheese, avocado, alfalfa and watercress are crammed thick and tight between two slices of multi-grain bread. The avocado is key. Without it, the sandwich would be too dry, but with it this sandwich is solid in taste and value.

The marketplace is stuffed with so many varieties of food that it's almost overwhelming. Everything from delicate little lime squares to a behemoth of a pizza-baked potato. Seating abounds upstairs where, although it's a little warm, they feature a corner-mounted television, a Coke machine and a Poland Springs water-cooler.

Daily Soup

Baked Potatoes, Sandwiches, Soup/Salad

241 W. 54th St. (bet. Broadway and Eighth Ave.)
Monday – Friday, 7 a.m. – 5 p.m.
(212) 765-SOUP

Daily Soup was the first and best known of the yuppie soup joints that exploded onto the scene in the '90's. As the soup craze cooled down, many of them folded, but Daily Soup is still ladling out a terrific menu of freshly made hot and cold delights.

The much beloved Blue Pot Special has gone the way of the dodo...but not really. The soups that used to rotate through the daily special are now all priced to move everyday. Nine soups are currently in the sub-five zone and come with a hunk of sourdough bread, a small oatmeal cookie and a choice of apple, orange or banana. These soups include Italian wedding, tomato and basil with tortellini, chicken noodle and turkey gumbo.

The fat-free vegetarian vegetable soup, despite its blandish name, is quite tasty and hearty. We gave up counting veggies after identifying broccoli, tomato, beans, peas and cauliflower. Daily Soup likes to rotate its soup selections daily, so you won't get bored. And by all means ask for a free taste of a few of the pricier soups. They want you to. It promotes sales.

The décor is distinctive and makes you feel like you're in a big industrial kitchen. Highly polished

39

metal surfaces everywhere. There's a long counter against one wall to eat on with plenty of tall chairs, which are cool enough to make up for them being awfully uncomfortable. At the end of the counter is a big pitcher of free water with orange slices floating on top. Pleasant tasting and a nice change of pace from the lemon water you find everywhere.

Daily Soup has diversified a bit as well. They now boast one of those omnipresent salad-made-to-order-bars as well as a baked potato bar. The potatoes are big and flavorful and one with chicken and cheese will only cost you $4.50. Classy Devon & Blakely is supplying them with baked goods and specialty sandwiches too. An attractive selection of sandwiches on rolls and baguettes include a number of $4.50 options. All these extras are certainly nice, but the core of their menu will always be great soup.

Devon & Blakely

Baked Potatoes, Soup/Salad

461 Fifth Ave. (bet. 40th and 41st streets)
Monday – Friday, 6:30 a.m. – 7 p.m.
Saturday, 8 a.m. – 5 p.m.
(212) 684-4321

If you frequent this establishment you may catch yourself calling the subway the "tube" or drinking tea with your pinky up. Devon & Blakely looks like it was created by some corporate catering cousin of Mary Poppins. Wood paneling, wicker baskets, full tea menu, attractive polished wood seating. Though you'd think that lunch on Fifth Avenue would only fit the budget of a Drummond or a silver spoon like Edward Straton III, less than $5 on Fifth is possible here. Maybe they got the currency conversion wrong.

In a lovely refrigerated display, they present several different specialty salads for $1.50 - $3 per quarter pound. Choices include German potato salad, pesto tortollini, various penne dishes and honey curry chicken. The Greek salad is tops with its flavorful spinach and huge pieces of crumbly Feta. They also serve five hearty soup choices daily. A small will run you $3.25, a large goes for $4.25. They do the free sample thing, so try them all. Despite the whole Boston Tea Party, they serve dynamite Boston Clam Chowder loaded with clams and flavor. Over by the tea menu, there's a build-your-own potato bar. D&B insists you tell them exactly what you'd like on yours. Chickpeas?

Scallions? Bacon? Broccoli? Yum. $2.45 for the spud, plus 50¢ – $1 per item.

D&B's spin on the create-your-own-salad craze starts with a choice of three different greens at $2.95 for a small or $3.95 for a large. Unless your name is Peter and you're routinely chased by Farmer MacGregor, go for the small and have them throw in a few goodies. Buyer beware: all items except dressing are à la carte! The charge is small though, between 25¢ and 75¢ for most items, and they don't skimp as they sling great tongs-full of salad yummies into the mix. At $3.95, a spinach salad tossed with balsamic vinaigrette and full of freshly sliced mushrooms and ripe tomatoes is deliciously filling.

Even the candy by the cashier is British. Where else in NYC can you get UK delights like Maltesers (Whoppers with an accent), the Nestle Lion bar or the awesome Crisp bar? The Brit bars are $1. Euros not accepted.

Famous Famiglia

Italian, Pizza

686 Eighth Ave. (bet. 43rd and 44th streets)
Seven days, 10 a.m. – 2 a.m.
(212) 382-3030

Famous Famiglia is a delicious and immaculately clean pizza place with a real community feel. Its walls are covered with framed letters from school groups, community outreach programs and even the mayor's office thanking them for donations to various charitable events or for their well-executed catering services. The warm fuzzies are great, but the food is even better.

The sauce, the soul of any pizza joint, is lip-smackingly delicious. Light and zippy, it tastes of ripe plum tomatoes. And the calzones are ridiculously good (starting at $3.75). Firm, delectable dough surrounds a one-two punch of cheeses: sweet ricotta on the bottom, rich mozzarella on top. Famous Famiglia is generous with the stuffings (cheese, pepperoni, broccoli, mushroom), and displays the calzones with a little piece of the stuffing crowning the dough. The pepperoni calzone, for example, has a little curl of pepperoni on top. It's cute.

The regular and gourmet slices will wow you too. The fresca slice, for example, with thin crispy crust, firm mozzarella, sweet basil and paper-thin slices of tomato, is well worth its $3.25 price tag.

There's a newborn in the famigilia at Broadway and 50th Street, with a Caffé Famiglia section and tons of seating, but we're loyal to the Eighth Avenue location. The whole place, including the display counter, is bright and clean with lots of patterned tile work and several pictures of the famiglia doing pizza things like flipping dough in Times Square or inspecting tomatoes together. The seating capacity is decent, with about 8 two-seater tables. They top all this off with genuinely excellent service. They might offer an extra side of red sauce without your having to ask. If someone sneezes, a "God bless you" can usually be heard coming from behind the counter. When you sit down at the table and unpack your food you might find a side of free garlic knots has come your way. Itsa nice. Itsa famiglia.

Figaro Restaurant & Bar

Pizza

26 W. 44th St. (bet. Fifth and Sixth avenues)
Monday – Saturday, 6:30 a.m. – 9 p.m.
(212) 840-1010

Figaro is an upscale bar with très chic ambiance. Manhattan themed murals, one of Central Park and the other of Rockefeller Center, adorn the walls, and a lovely second floor loft overlooks the main seating area. Figaro obviously caters to an expense account clientele and not one entrée, pizza, sandwich or pasta on the menu is less than $5. So don't order off the menu!

Those in the know without much dough eschew the menu and get slices of pizza, priced at just $1.60 plus 65¢ for each topping. To snag one, blow past the maitre d' to the back of the restaurant where you'll find a glass paneled pizza counter. There, as you revel in the sweet smell of dough and marinara, they'll hook you up. Weighing in slightly larger than a typical New York slice, their slices begin life as cheese only. You tell them which of the more than twenty toppings you'd like, and they pile it on and pop it in the oven. (The crabmeat topping will cost you a little extra.) While the meat toppings are cooked through, the vegetables tend to be undercooked or even raw. It's like salad on your 'za: crunchy and light. The pizza itself has a bold flavor and features a thick and tangy sauce.

You'll need to skip the tables in the main and loft

(continued)

areas if you're eating slices, however. Figaro reserves them for menu service. You're welcome, though, to enjoy your tasty frugality at one of the much cooler bar tables up front. There, you also get a better view of the street, televisions and murals.

"Nothing spoils lunch any quicker than a rogue meatball rampaging through your spaghetti."

JIM DAVIS

Food Emporium

Market/Grocery, Sushi

**NE Corner of 49th Street and Eighth Avenue
24 hours a day, Monday 7 a.m. – Sunday 12 a.m.
(212) 977-1710**

A grocery store is one of the last places you'd think of as a hopping locale for the business luncher. So why do so many choose The Emporium? Aside from the Siren allure of their fingers-on-the-chalkboard jingle "Food Emporium! Food Emporium!", this haphazardly operated grocery store cooks up one of the finest half roasted chicken specials in Times Square.

For merely $2.99/lb, the Food Emporium's hungry man special (our name, not theirs) is so hearty that the obligatory 75¢ bag of chips is not necessary (but recommended nevertheless)! Check it out: a half pound bird comes dripping with grease in a tightly sealed container with a small pedestal on which the chicken is perched, thusly allowing the grease to thankfully drip off. The white meat easily falls off the bone, and is as moist as you'll find under a heat lamp. So juicy is the chicken, you can tear off the wing and thigh, making a fork and knife optional. And at such a low price per pound, there's no reason that you can't enjoy a larger bird, if one pound of fowl won't satisfy your appetite.

If chicken isn't your desire, Food Emporium has other options: standard pre-packaged deli salads, reasonably priced chicken rolls ($4.25) and slices of pizza ($1.49). Although we found the sushi pretty standard, Food Emporium's customers must think differently. There's a daily gathering for the $3.99 specials, which usually combine a meat and vegetable, like shrimp and cucumber rolls, or spicy tuna with California rolls.

Even if you don't need a caffeine fix, settle into Eight O'Clock Coffee, located inside the Emporium, where you'll find a few counter seats where you can eat your lunch. As you lunch, you'll be treated to the tasty aroma of fresh brewed coffee, and this thought: "I'm gorging on rotisserie chicken at a grocery store coffee counter with a view of Starbucks across the street...only in New York."

Fresco Tortillas

Mexican

125 W. 42nd St. (bet. Sixth Avenue and Broadway)
Monday – Friday, 11 a.m. – 9 p.m.
Saturday – Sunday, 12 p.m. – 9 p.m.
(212) 221-5849
(212) 221-1918

The creation of Chinese immigrants Rose and Desni Zheng, Fresco Tortillas is a visual paradox that exemplifies New York's cultural diversity: a Chinese staff running a Tex-Mex restaurant. And while some argue it's not "real" Mexican food, they can't argue about the taste and service. Of all the places like it in NYC (and there are a lot), Fresco is the best. You could blindfold yourself, throw a dart at the menu and be happy.

The menu features more than 50 selections (just like this book): tacos, quesadillas, enchiladas, burritos and more. There are tons of vegetarian choices and plenty of items for less than $2. The specialty of the house is the fresh flour tortilla, which is made quite simply. Start with a small clump of dough, throw it into a flattening device, toss it onto the grill and voila! You've now got a fresh tortilla that tantalizes the taste buds with its warm flavor and the powdery remains of rolling flour.

The black bean and cheese tortilla is a staple, and at 99¢, there's no reason not to enjoy its cheesy goodness. Avocado lovers will relish the over-stuffed guacamole tortilla. The sliced meat in the steak taco is tender and grilled medium. And while the Tex-Mex chili con carne tortilla is a little heavy, it has a nice down-home smoky kick. The rich and famous can feast on one of the tostada salads served in a crisp flour tortilla bowl, but unless you choose the black bean ($4.29), it'll just burst your $5 budget.

Fresco further distinguishes itself with lightning-quick service. By the time you pay the cashier your $4 and change, your food should be ready to be taken kitty-corner to Bryant Park. You can eat in, but the cavernous room was painted a shocking pink years ago and the ambiance feels more like old-school 42nd street from the Koch years, rather than the cleaned up Disney-fied street of Guiliani's term.

Golden Chicken Ribs & Steak

Southern, Steaks

604 Ninth Ave. (bet. 43rd and 44th streets)
Seven days, 11 a.m. – 12 a.m.
(212) 245-8790

Golden Chicken Ribs & Steak is so good you'll be licking your fingers for a week. It doesn't look like much from the outside, but the inside...isn't much better; imagine how Elvis would decorate a rib shack if he were still alive and broke. But it's reasonably clean and they have the best cheap ribs in town.

For $4.85 (prices include tax) you get a quarter rack of baby back pork ribs which are fall-off-the-bone tender. The lip-smacking sauce is tangy sweet with lots of molasses in the mix, and at the tables they arm you with a decent BBQ sauce and a very good two-alarm hot sauce. The only thing missing? That catchy doo-wop group from Chili's. The rib deal comes with choice of roll or pita (the pita's better) and a choice of one of their many excellent hot and cold sides. They run this deal with chicken too, but for 25¢ less: same extras, but a quarter chicken (white or dark meat) instead of the ribs. The chicken is great and a nice option for non-rib eaters. If you like the other white meat, however, make like their food and stick to the ribs.

The menu boasts more sides then the Social Security debate and on any given day they have about 10 hot and cold sides competing for atten-tion. Hots include corn on the cob, French fries, mac and cheese, homemade chicken soup, creamed spinach and sweet raisin cinnamon apples. Colds include many salads including Greek, potato, red kidney bean and cole slaw. If you can't decide on one, try this: any three small sides for $4.95, a great meal in itself.

Including the ribs and chicken, they have more than 20 "main courses" for less than $5 ranging from fried shrimp to hamburgers to salad pita sandwiches to their latest addition, pizza. Where else in midtown can you get a BBQ roast beef sandwich with lettuce and tomato plus a side of mac and cheese for only $4.95 AND not have to worry about a tip?

Halal Food

Middle Eastern, Street-cart

**South side of 55th Street (west of Sixth Avenue)
Monday – Saturday, 11 a.m. – 5 p.m.**

The sign in front of this nameless Middle Eastern street-cart reads "If you like the food, tell your friends…If not, tell us." Well we're telling you, aren't we?

The gyro is dynamite ($3.50). Nice and juicy, but wrapped so expertly that it's not too much of a mess. They slice the meat off that big rotating cylinder of lamb (vertical spit roasting) and take their time searing it up on the grill. It's their vegetable mix, however, that really puts this sandwich over the top. They somehow stuff a serving of a delicious mixture of broccoli, carrots and onion inside the pita with the lamb and top it off with traditional gyro sauce. It's lamb stew in a pita for a song.

The only problem here is deciding whether to go for the gyro or the chicken. The chicken pita (also $3.50) contains an abundance of tender juicy chicken. That alone is not uncommon for this type of street-cart. Again, however, their veggy-mix bumps it up a notch. Maybe they have no name in order to guard their vegetable recipe like Coke guards its secret formula. Ancient Halal secret.

The homemade hot sauce should be respected but not feared. Reasonably hot, but very flavorful, it draws out the flavor of the meats rather than simply incinerating the lining of your esophagus.

This anonymous street-cart is usually parked between a similarly unnamed hotdog cart and a falafel stand on the south side of 55th Street just west of Sixth Avenue.

"Democracy is two wolves and a lamb voting on what to have for lunch."

BENJAMIN FRANKLIN

Hale and Hearty Soups

Soup/Salad

49 W. 42nd St. (east of Sixth Avenue)
Monday – Friday, 10:30 a.m. – 6 p.m.
(212) 575-9090

Aren't "hale" and "hearty" synonyms? It's like calling Anna Nicole Smith tacky and tawdry. Enough nitpicking, though. The soup is good, the salads are even better and everyone knows it because the place is nutso crowded.

We under-fivers can manage a large cup ($2.95) or a bowl ($3.75) of one of their six everyday soups. Of those, both the 10 vegetable and the green and yellow split pea are souper (sorry, had to be done); the chicken vegetable and gazpacho are good; the Tucsan white bean and three-lentil chili, however, are on the bland side. They've got plenty of exotic soups like Senegalese chicken, mulligatawny and chilled Indian pear, but if you want to be a fancypants, you'll need to get a small portion to stay less than $5. They've got those cute little tasting cups, so taste a couple of the chic soups and then go for the good 'n cheap stuff.

Realizing that the winter soup craze melts as temperatures rise, they also boast an outstanding made-to-order salad counter. Stand in line with all the twenty-somethings trying not to turn into their parents and grab some roughage. Some toppings are free (cukes, carrot, onions, croutons) and some will >gasp< cost you extra, such as mushrooms, grilled chicken or tuna. Their eight salad dressings are all winners with the standouts being an electrifying fat-free carrot ginger and a sinus-zapping honey mustard.

Hale and Hearty clearly labels their vegetarian, low fat and dairy-free soups and all soups (and salads) come with a hunk of bread or a sack of oysterettes. Don't even think about trying to sit there during the lunch crunch of 12 p.m. – 2 p.m. It's a hassle eating with butts and elbows pressed against you on every side. Depending on which location you're at (there's another one at 55 W. 56th St. between Fifth and Sixth avenues), hop it over to either Bryant Park or Central Park. Who knows, maybe you'll meet someone special and you can spend all that cash you saved on him or her. Isn't Anna Nicole single these days?

Hallo Berlin

German, Hot Dogs/Sausages, Street-cart

North side of 54th Street (west of Fifth Avenue)
Tuesday – Friday, 11 a.m. – 5 p.m.
*Closed the entire month of July

The "Wurst pushcart in NY!" was created in the early '70's when Rolf Babiel, a German immigrant construction worker, got fed up with the tepid watery excuses for hot dogs he found at New York street-carts. So he began his own stand serving real imported German wursts, and more than 20 years and three restaurants later, he still runs the cart because "It's fun."

The menu uses German car codewords for each of its nine varieties of wurst. Order a BMW and an Audi, for example, and you're eating Bavarian-lite weisswurst and bauernwurst. If that means as much to you as it does to us, don't worry, Rolf'll give you the lowdown on what's in what. Order a wurst alone ($2.50 – $3.50) and you'll get it served in a warm crusty roll with imported cabbage, onion and a very smooth spicy mustard. The wursts' flavors range from mild to intense and are exceptionally well complemented by the garnishes.

For $5, you can upgrade to one of Rolf's "Soul" Food Combo Mixes. The "Freakin' Special" is your choice of wurst, German potato salad and a Bavarian meatball. The potato salad is chilled and flecked with dill, and the meatball is a good mouthful and great with the mustard. Or try the "Dictator Special", bratwurst and Berliner wurst (no

57

choices with the dictator, of course), onions, cabbage, roll and German potatoes.

This inimitable cart is addictively delicious and gets equal points for freshness, flavor and distinctiveness. What an amazing break from the lunchtime norm.

Rolf is a natural salesman who clearly loves what he does and prides himself on delivering the highest quality food and service to his fiercely devoted patrons. His custom cart near St. Patrick's Cathedral and Rockefeller Center is decked out with side counters (with red-checked tablecloths no less) on which to place your food, and a nasty looking metal contraption bolted to the front. What is it? Change dispenser? Torture device? We asked Rolf just as he was getting our wursts ready and, with a gleam in his eye, he dropped our sausages into the contraption, pulled its slot-machine arm, and instantly sliced the wursts into bite sized bits! As we stood there agape, he smiled and stated simply but proudly..."German engineering."

Hello Deli

Burgers, Sandwiches

213 W. 53rd St. (bet. Broadway and Eighth Ave.)
Monday – Friday, 7 a.m. – 5 p.m.
Saturday, 7 a.m. – 3 p.m.
(212) 489-7832

Hello Deli is a clean little hole-in-the-wall, crammed with run-down tables and chairs. Ordinarily, delis such as this go unnoticed, but Hello Deli is literally next door to the stage entrance of the Ed Sullivan Theatre where *The Late Show with David Letterman* tapes. In 1994, Hello Deli became an overnight sensation when Letterman aired a sketch called "Fun with Rupert", making a star of Deli owner Rupert Jee. Rupert became an unlikely celebrity and his store became a tourist stop almost as popular as Carnegie or Katz's Deli...but a whole lot cheaper.

The greatest values are in the vegetarian part of the menu where a veggie pocket, vegetarian club or veggie burger will land you in less than $5 land. The green giant pita, while not living up to its name in size, does so in taste. Raw crunchy veggies are tempered by sautéed mushrooms, onions and peppers in this sandwich topped off with melted cheese. The Pat Farmer ($2.95) is a delicious veggie burger with lettuce, tomato, cucumber yogurt and honey mustard. This unusual combo is stacked high on a bakery style bun and is more filling than you'd think; a Pat F. with cheese and a twenty ounce bottle of Coke rings in, after tax, at $5 even, Steven.

Hello Deli, of course, pays homage to their patron saint Dave Letterman with Dave's Hoagie, which is turkey, ham, cheese, lettuce, tomato, oil and vinegar on a hero. Located in the theatre district, they usually name a sandwich after the show playing across the street at the Broadway Theatre. Even though it closed in 2000, they still have the *Miss Saigon*: a triple-decker turkey, cheese, lettuce and tomato sandwich. Chicken Parmigiana, a cheeseburger with fries and a salad are all wallet friendly lunches at Hello Deli. Other good bets are grilled cheese ($2.75), grilled Swiss with tuna and tomato ($4), egg salad ($3.25) and good old PB&J ($2).

Whatever your preference, Rupert will be there smiling, taking orders and usually building the sandwiches himself. He's always happy to pose for a picture with a customer or to help Dave horribly embarrass you on national TV.

Hot Dog King

Hot Dogs/Sausages, Street-cart

SW corner of 49th Street and Sixth Avenue
Monday – Saturday, 11 a.m. – 5 p.m.

All hail his Royal Highness the Hot Dog King who doth most tastily grill his dogs. See, most vendors boil their hot dogs, which results too often in damp, flimsy and flavorless dogs that may soggify your bun (think Wonder Bread soaked in tepid dishwater). The King, however, grills his dogs just like you do in your own backyard or like they do at that Vietnamese place down the street. What that gets you is a plump juicy crispy-on-the-outside hot dog served on a warm grilled bun.

His royal repertoire also includes spicy hot beef sausages, excellent pretzels and scrumptious knishes. As a rule, street-cart knishes are poor cousins to the "real" knishes found in mid-to-upscale delis, but the King's are the exception. Though he starts with the same brand as the other venders, his knishes are delicious. Maybe it's because he lets them crisp up real nice on the side of the grill.

The King's technique adds to his mystique. Note how he slices the dog lengthwise in one fluid motion before applying mustard Picasso-like with a brush. The aforementioned knishes do not escape the King's blade; watch him slice a deep pocket into the steamy spud-bomb and fill 'er up with spicy mustard. (Note: the King tends to be

(continued)

generous with the mustard, so if mega-mustard ain't your style, ask him to go light.) Oh, by the way, not a single item at his courtly cart is more than $1.25. You can stuff yourself with a jumbo hot dog, a hot sausage, a pretzel or a knish and a can of soda for $5 at this most regal food wagon. Huzzah! Long live the Hot Dog King!

"Let not the sands of time get in your lunch."

NATIONAL LAMPOON

House of Pita (HOP)

Kosher, Middle Eastern

32 W. 48th St. (bet. Fifth and Sixth avenues)
Monday – Thursday, 6:30 a.m. – 5:30 p.m.
Friday, 6:30 a.m. – 2:30 p.m.
(212) 391-4242

You'd expect this tiny Glatt Kosher take-out establishment to be frequented by Hassidic diamond
merchants, and it is. But where did everyone else
come from? Blue-collars, cabbies, suits and tourists
struggling to pronounce "falafel" are all there
enjoying the House of Pita's tasty offerings. Who
knew a good blintz could bring us all together?

The falafel ($4) is very good and, we know this
sounds crazy, refreshing! Maybe it's their liberal
use of parsley, or the ratio of the shredded lettuce
and tomato to the deep fried crispies. The potato
pancakes ($1.25), while flavorful, suffer from heat-
lampitis; only get one if they're freshly fried.
They've got a zillion different salads and, if you
ask, they'll pack two or three into a single half-
pound to-go container ($3.50). This way you get a
nice filling sampling dish without blowing your
bankroll on one item. They make a nice tabuli
using just enough oil and lemon to moisten it up.
The white-cabbage salad is great; it's Jewish
coleslaw really: shredded cabbage, fresh parsley,
oil and vinegar.

HOP's blintzes should be marketed by Hostess and
carry a diabetic warning! The wrap is twice the

thickness of a crepe and three times as sweet. In the middle lurks what seems like a gallon of sweet-sour cheese filling, which tastes similar to ricotta cheese. Delicious, but for sweet-tooths only.

Half the fun is getting there. Located at the end of an arcade tunnel running between 47th and 48th streets (about halfway between Sixth and Fifth avenues), The HOP's formal address is 32 West 48th St. But it's far more fun to walk the arcade starting on 47th street. Though you can sit at the one stool at HOP, the counter is oompa-loompa sized and directly next to the trash can, so get your grub to go.

John's

Sandwiches, Steaks, Street-cart

NE corner of 56th Street and Seventh Avenue
Monday – Saturday, 11 a.m. – 5 p.m.

John's menu is what stops you in your tracks. A rib-eye steak sandwich for only $4.50? Impressive. Then you remember that you're at a street-cart and it really gets interesting. So you order the rib-eye sandwich, fully expecting some shaved gray meat on a stale bun, and they open up a cooler and pull out a lovely, albeit thin, cut of rib-eye on butcher paper! They grill and wrap this beauty in a warm pita; stuff the sandwich with stingingly raw onion, lettuce and tomato; and top off the whole thing with a tangy white sauce. Trust us on this; it's even better than it sounds.

John used to serve an amazing mozzarella and prosciutto sandwich. Sadly, costs went up and it wasn't selling, so the coach had to cut it from the lineup. While we lobby for its return, enjoy his excellent lamb kabob in a pita ($3.50). John usually shakes a little salt on the grill before slapping the pita down to warm. This salt encrusted wrapper turns on your saliva jets as you tear into the tender pieces of lamb within. Lettuce, tomato, white sauce and hot sauce are the accessories of choice for this one, folks.

Though the two eastern European entrepreneurs who run this stand are the new kids on the block of Sixth Avenue street-cart vendors, they wouldn't

(continued)

be out of line if they doubled their current prices; the food's that good. They also serve platter lunches: $5 for steak and $4.50 for chicken. They use Kingsford brand charcoal for their grill which, according to all the Kingsford commercials, must be why their food tastes so good. We have a sneaking suspicion, however, that the freshness and high quality of their ingredients may have a little something to do with it too.

"Anyone who has lost track of time when using a computer knows the propensity to dream, the urge to make dreams come true and the tendency to miss lunch."

TIM BERNERS-LEE

Kwik Meal

Sandwiches, Street-cart

SW corner of 45th Street and Sixth Avenue
Monday – Saturday, 11 a.m. – 5 p.m.

Kwik Meal looks like the lovechild of a hotdog cart and an RV. Towering above the lunch crowds and its competitors, it boasts side shelves for your food as well as a broad canopy to shelter you from the sun or rain while you contemplate its varied menu. It's tough to tell which is brighter: the gleaming chrome of the walls or the friendly smiles of the owners, a husband and wife team. She takes the orders and cash while he does the cooking sporting a huge white puffy chef's hat. You can watch him do his grilling thing through a transparent Plexiglas shield on his end of the mega-cart.

When asked what their specialty is, they immediately respond "lamb kabob" in stereo and we couldn't agree more. The lamb kabob pita ($5) is superb. Decidedly not a gyro (you know, in which the lamb is sliced off the big lamb-cylinder-thing), this wonderful pita is stuffed with delicately seasoned flash-grilled chunks of tender lamb nestled in sweet grilled onions and a not-too-tangy yogurt sauce. They also serve a mean chicken kabob pita ($4), a veggie pita ($3) and a steak and cheese sandwich ($4), as well as more common street-cart fare like hotdogs and knishes. They display a great selection of beverages including A&W Root Beer, Lipton Iced Tea, Snapple, Coke, Pepsi and Sprite behind more Plexiglas on the wide front of the cart.

We gotta mention that they also serve a pastrami sandwich, a very rare street-cart offering, for an ultra-low $4. He grills the pastrami up and serves it on a short hero roll with a little spicy mustard and bread-and-butter pickles. Though it's good for its price and while we applaud pastrami's entrance into the street-cart arena, it's not their best. Stick with the lamb kabob.

Until recently, Kwik Meal's name was Kwik Meal #5. When asked why they dropped the number, the chef replied "Too many people asking where the other four were!"

Lemon Tree Café

Middle Eastern

769 Ninth Ave. (bet. 51st and 52nd streets)
Seven days, 11 a.m. – 11 p.m.
(212) 245-0818

Lemon Tree Café is far and away the best all-around Middle Eastern restaurant in its price range. They serve everything a Middle Eastern street-cart does at about the same price. Everything on their menu, however, comes with walls, a ceiling, tables, chairs and relaxed service at no extra charge, except a tip, of course.

Their babaganoush ($3.25 for sandwich or side) is mellow and flavorful without the burning acidity of some 'ganoushes, and their hummus ($3 sandwich or side) is good and garlicky without too much oil. Their falafel is delicious, but make sure it's fresh out of the fryer; it gets gummy if it's been sitting around for a while.

Their sandwiches are filling and served in a basket on pita with tomato, crisp red cabbage and tihini. Choices include falafel, hummus, babaganoush, shish kabob, chicken cutlet, shawerma and kefta. And if you left your culinary passport at home, you can get a burger on a pita plus fries for $4.25. Can't decide? Get a combo like the babaganoush and falafel sandwich. This is the McDLT of Middle Eastern cuisine with the cool smooth eggplant squaring off against the hot crispiness of the chickpeas. A steal at $3.75.

Beyond the hummus and babaganoush, they've got more unusual items like lahmajune (Middle Eastern pizza) and ejji (a type of omelet). Skip the kibbi, an unusual but bland deep fried cone of crushed wheat filled with ground beef. The spinach pie ($1.50), however, is the best we've ever had. Several flaky sheets of dough surround an amazing spinach stuffing. It's not your standard quiche-like spinach middle. It's more like an outstanding spinach sauté with sweet chopped onion and a hint of lemon and oil.

Lemon Tree has a Middle Eastern bohemian thing going on. Garage sale art on the walls and vertical mirrored stripes alternating with shiny wood paneling everywhere. They seat about 30 and the atmosphere is cool, dim and relaxed.

Margon Restaurant

Cuban, Sandwiches

136 W. 46th St. (bet. Broadway and Sixth Ave.)
Monday – Friday, 6 a.m. – 5 p.m.
Saturday, 6 a.m. – 2:30 p.m.
(212) 354-5013

You have no choice but to get cozy with your neighbors at Margon, where lines stream out the door and finding a seat is as easy as a woman getting a membership at Augusta. With a clientele as culturally diverse as the 2012 New York Olympics, Margon is everything this book celebrates; delicious, cheap and distinctive.

This throwback luncheonette is split into two sections. In the back where they have seating for 25, you can order one of the daily specials like ox tail, tripe with pig feet or octopus salad. These delicious specials tragically run at least $6, however. Anyway, it's a pain to wade through the mass of humanity waiting to get back there.

So skip that sweaty mambo and park yourself upfront on a stool at the sandwich counter where they serve delectable grilled pressed sandwiches. Ham and cheese, steak, pernil and tuna fish are four of Margon's six sandwich selections for less than $5; the other two get more ink below.

The specialty of the house is (naturally) the Cuban sandwich ($4), which, when combined with a $1 can of soda, makes the quintessential $5 lunch.

A Cuban sandwich comes stacked with hot ham, pork, salami, cheese and pickles. A few squirts of hot sauce are highly recommended. First-timers may find the flavor a little intense, however.

If the Cuban sandwich is too much for your delicate palate, order the chicken ($4); you won't be disappointed. Sliced off the bone then and there and served on grilled Italian bread, the chicken is infused with paprika and comes with your choice of mayo, mustard or hot sauce. Throw on a slice of cheese if you please for an extra buck.

There's really no going wrong at Margon. On one of our last trips there, a customer exclaimed to his friend "It's just like I'm back in Miami." Yeah, but without all the annoying pastels.

Mee Noodle Shop & Grill

Chinese

795 Ninth Ave. (SW corner of 53rd Street)
Sunday – Thursday, 11:30 a.m. – 11:30 p.m.
Friday – Saturday, 11:30 a.m. – 12:30 a.m.
(212) 765-2929
(212) 765-2982

Manhattan is swarming with so many Chinese restaurants it's quite difficult to distinguish one from another. With so many of them sub-par, you have to love Mee Noodle Shop & Grill, with its gargantuan selection of colorful and flavorful dishes.

Since Mee's menu offers more than 350 options, it's no surprise to find numerous choices for less than $5. You may opt for one of the ten special platters offered anytime for $4.25. Or, starting at 11:30 a.m. everyday, enjoy one of the lunch specials that are generously available until 5 p.m. There are more than twenty-five specials for $4.25 – $4.50, and each comes with a free egg roll or soup. If you opt for the lunch special, we recommend the crispy egg roll or flavorsome wonton soup over the disappointingly bland hot and sour soup.

When deciding on a main dish, keep this in mind: at Mee's, the sauce dominates. The brown sauce is extremely rich and quizzically sticky. As a result, it clings to the ingredients and blends its strong flavor to every bite. The garlic sauce, thinner than the brown, delivers a sweet zing to its dishes. And if you're a sweet and sour lover, take note that Mee's is extra vinegary.

One oddity. Mee shreds its beef (à la shredded beef Schezuan-style) in many dishes where you wouldn't expect it: beef with string beans, for example. If that's something that would bother you, ask about it when ordering.

The portions at Mee are generous, and the décor is eclectic. The staff is easy going and seemingly psychic, attentively bringing extra plates and sauces to the table before you realize they're needed. No matter how you slice it, Mee delivers, both literally and figuratively.

Minar Indian Restaurant

Indian

138 W. 46th St. (bet. Sixth and Seventh avenues)
Monday – Saturday, 10:30 a.m. – 7:30 p.m.
(212) 398-4600

The Mahatma would have had a tough time sticking to a hunger fast here. Minar serves an enormous variety of inexpensive Indian dishes to a mostly Indian clientele. The food is delicious, authentic and non-violent – well I guess a food fight could break out if they ran out of Roti.

Freebies abound. The tables are each topped by a pitcher of free water (cups by the cahier). Meals come with choice of rice or the aforementioned Roti, which is an Indian pita-type bread that tastes like matzah that has been allowed to rise. You also get a gratis side salad served with a cool yogurt dressing.

The dishes range from simple navrattan vegetable curry ($4.50) and alu matar (potatoes and green peas cooked Punjabi style, $4.50) to more unusual dishes (well, to us anyway) like matar paneer: a mixture of peas and lightly fried cheese cubes cooked in a lightly spiced curry.

If Popeye frequented the sub-continent, he'd fill up on the Tuesday special, saag sarso da ($4.50). Saag looks like a serving of steakhouse creamed spinach, but its flavor is more complex. More smooth than creamy, the concoction includes onions and spices which give the saag a deep flavor with a very subtle heat.

Minar serves a beautiful dosa, the Indian version of a crepe. While some are soft and stuffed like a tortilla, others are sweet-smelling sculptures: golden brown cylinders of starch daring you to violate their perfect shapes with a bite or a tear. Sada dosa ($3.95) is made out of rice and lentil flour and rava dosa ($4.95) is thinner, crispier and made out of wheat, rice and onions.

"I believe that you got upholstered at lunch."

ANDY, *WKRP IN CINCINNATI*

Moshe's

Kosher, Middle Eastern, Sandwiches, Street-cart
South side of 46th Street (east of Sixth Avenue)
Monday – Friday, 11 a.m. – 5 p.m.
* Fridays, they close well before sundown.

Moshe (moh-sheh) is the Hebrew name for Moses. You know, Charlton Heston with the crazy hair and beard and all. In Yiddish, however, it rhymes with oy, as in M'oy-this-is-good!-sheh. If Moshe's falafel stand were around during the Exodus, the children of Israel would have forgotten about Canaan and headed straight to the diamond district.

It's all about the falafel here, folks. They've got other stuff, but why bother? For $4.25 you get a can of soda and the best falafel we've had in the United States. The sandwich is enormous and is an exercise in food architecture. They start with a few crispy deep fried falafel balls in the bottom of the pita and mash them down to form a stable base. Then they pile on layer after layer of lettuce, tomato, onion and of course, tons more falafel. We really want to convey the sheer weight of this sandwich...two pounds, three? Geez, we just don't know, we'll have to bring a scale next time.

Topping off the sandwich are a few more balls and a few choices to make: tahini, hot sauce and pick-les. The cool tahini sauce is almost a requirement; a falafel sandwich minus tahini would be like tuna salad without mayo: desert dry. Their hot sauce is major league, so for most falafelers ordering it with "a little hot sauce" will be sufficient. The pickles are

77

tiny little gherkins with a briny sharp kick: delicious, but not the standard dill you're probably used to.

You must be clear about what you want. This stand is insanely busy and loud at lunchtime, so have your order ready to bellow out. Here's Eddie's usual, for example, "Falafel, everything, little bit of hot sauce, extra pickle, extra pickle!"

Now whatever you do, don't eat two! It is very common for Moshe's novices to become delusional from the deliciousness and think they can eat two falafel sandwiches with no consequences; this is pure hubris. It's just too much. Please trust us on this. (Besides, two would be more than $5 ;-)

Moshe's holds a special place in our hearts, and in the arteries and veins leading to and from our hearts. With that in mind, let us leave you with our lyrical tribute to the progenitor of this guide (sung to the tune of Starship's *Sara*).

Moshe's, Moshe's
You're so deliciously glatt.
Moshe's, Moshe's
We're sad when you're not there on Shabbat.

New Era Café

Bakery, Sandwiches, Soup/Salad

Rockefeller Concourse Subway Area
  (directly below 49th Street and Sixth Avenue)
Monday – Friday, 6 a.m. – 9 p.m.
Saturday, 7 a.m. – 7 p.m.
(212) 581-5952

This long bakery counter underneath Rockefeller Center is great for a tasty lunch built on fresh baked goods. There's no seating, but you can eat at a standup counter or, better yet, take your food down the hall to the impressive seating area at the north end of the underground Rockefeller Concourse.

At $2.50, the half-sandwiches make great lunch centerpieces. Most days they have a pile of pre-mades ready to grab, but if you don't see what you like, ask and they'll make it fresh. You get one main ingredient, and they stock all the standards: turkey, roast beef, tuna and ham. Lettuce and tomato are free as are any of their spreads; in addition to the staples (mayo, mustard, ketchup), you can also opt for pesto. Sure, it's just half a sandwich, but the thick slabs of fresh bread they serve it on make it delicious and filling. And check out the choices: French baguette, sourdough, country French, Italian semolina, whole wheat, rye (seeded or plain), pane rustico, ciabatta rustico, seven grain and challah (with or without raisins)!

They ladle out four varieties of soup every day

(small $2.75 / large $3.50), which are served with a choice of several different mini-loafs. You'll also get a mini if you opt for a meal-sized garden or Caesar salad.

They've got about a jillion different kinds of inexpensive baked goods to round out your meal. Rule of thumb: heat 'em before you eat 'em. Unless you're lucky enough to get something right out of the oven, ask them to zap your chocolate cigar, corn muffin, apricot coffee ring, prune danish or broccoli and cheese croissant (just to name a few). The apple turnover, for example, is pleasant at room temperature; but hot, it's a bona fide flaky gooey treat. After all, the only thing better than carbs and sugar is warm carbs and sugar.

New York Popover

Popovers, Sandwiches

789 Ninth Ave. (bet. 52nd and 53rd streets)
Seven days, 7:30 a.m. – 11 p.m.
(646) 746-0312
www.nypopover.com

If Bengal Express, one of our favorite cheap Indian restaurants, had to go, at least it was replaced by this fantastic new café. Out with the curry, in with the popover, as the saying goes. Popovers, which are a New England creation, are fist-sized boulders of baked dough made in muffin tins. When cooked, they "pop-up" creating an incredibly light and airy treat. Their slightly sweet popover contains no butter or oil, is made with skim milk, and lends itself very well to sandwiches and desserts alike.

For $1.65 you get a plain popover, which you can then accessorize à la carte from the varied list of "poppings" (groan), most of which are $1.35. Vegetable poppings include: grilled onions and peppers, grilled zucchini, roasted garlic, sautéed mushrooms, sautéed spinach, steamed broccoli and fresh tomatoes. Stuffed into a steaming split popover, sautéed spinach and mushrooms make a delicious combination: slightly salty, generously portioned and piping hot ($4.35).

For carnivores, they'll stuff a sandwich with grilled chicken, ham, prosciutto, roast beef, roasted or smoked turkey, bacon, sausage or chili. The smoked turkey is savory and sliced thin. They also have plenty of cheeses to choose from: extra sharp cheddar, feta, fontina, Monterey Jack, Swiss and brie. Premium items like asparagus, sun-dried tomatoes and fresh mozzarella are yummy but will cost you an extra 50¢ each.

The sandwiches are distinctive and delish, but desserts are where New York Popover really excels. Just think about hot dough filled with strawberries and whipped cream, or warm sliced apple compote. They serve plenty of fancy desserts, but it's hard to beat the simple delight of a popover with powdered sugar and lemon ($3).

New York Popover's good taste extends beyond its menu to its décor. Small candleholders are perched on dark wooden counters running the length of the exposed brick walls, which ascend to a pressed tin ceiling. Seating is limited, but they've done well with the space they have.

This place seems to be more than a doughy gim-mick, folks. Let's keep it around; pop over and eat.

Nick's

Sandwiches, Street-cart
SE corner of 54th Street and Sixth Avenue
Monday – Saturday, 11 a.m. – 5 p.m.

Nick's street-cart serves a mean spicy chicken sandwich, if you can get past Nick's banter. It goes something like this – YOU: I'll have a chilidog. NICK: Don't have chili today. YOU: When will you have it? NICK: When it's cold! YOU: It's 25 degrees out. NICK: What can you do?

So forget about the chilidog and take in the specialty of the house, the spicy chicken ($4). As your meat cooks for about five minutes (lengthy in the street-cart world), Nick's assistant/maître d' escorts you to, as Nick puts it, "table 4". Table 4 is in fact the steps of the office building a few feet south of the cart. The table, maître d' and genteel service are all at once tongue-in-cheek, entertaining and very helpful. Nick's sidekick brings over your chicken when it's ready, as well as a much-needed stack of napkins. Then Nick himself steps over with a fork. Nick: You'll need this.

Finally, it's time to enjoy the succulent thick pieces of tahini-drenched chicken served in a pita. There are lots of flavorful trimmings: thick juicy slices of tomato, crispy raw onions, cool shredded lettuce, a variety of mixed spices and a choice of mild or hot sauce.

Just as you're finishing the juicy sandwich, Nick's

buddy is there with spare napkins for the mess you've made of your hands. Nick's so cool, he doesn't even ask you to pay until you're done with your meal. As you rise from the stone slab that is table 4, the maître d' is back with (we're dead serious) a toothpick for those stray bits of see-food. At Nick's, your lunch money gets you great food and hilariously great service. All this, and never a single solicitation for a tip. So remember your waitstaff on the way out.

> "My soul never thinks of beginning to wake up for other people till lunch-time."

MARY A. ARNIM

9th Avenue Cheese Market

Market/Grocery, Sandwiches

615 Ninth Ave. (bet. 43rd and 44th streets)
Monday – Saturday, 9 a.m. – 8 p.m.
Sunday, 10 a.m. – 7 p.m.
(212) 397-4700

Wooden barrels, candy without English on the
wrappers, and a free ranging cat make the 9th
Avenue Cheese Market feel more like France or
Holland than Hell's Kitchen. Then there's the
cheese: blocks, wedges and tubes of more colors,
smells and tastes than you can keep track of.

This small market is big on variety with approximately 50 kinds of fresh coffee beans and a
veritable United Nations of cheeses. Many of
them cost more than your typical Kraft single,
though. A pound of Holland Cow's Milk Aged
Raw Milk Gouda will set you back $22.99!

They do a brisk lunch business, offering more than
25 different sandwiches daily, all of which are only
$3.99 plus tax. And this ain't bologna and American
cheese on Wonder bread either. One of the real
standouts is the brie and sun-dried tomato with
balsamic vinegar, pine nut oil and walnut oil on an
onion sourdough baguette. The mellow brie and
the rich nut oils blend wonderfully with the sharper
flavors of the sun-dried tomato and onion.

And whether you are vegetarian, watching your
cholesterol or a meat-and-cheese kind of guy,

9th Avenue has a sandwich screaming your name.
Check out some of the choices: smoked salmon
and chive cream cheese on black Russian bread,
Genoa salami and spicy smoked gouda on a
French baguette, Saga blue cheese and roasted red
pepper on a roll, prosciutto and provolone with
arrugula, tomato, non-cholesterol mayo and Dijon
mustard on a baguette or smoked mozzarella and
eggplant on a baguette (and that's just a selection).

For you bread haters out there, they do the pre-
portioned deli salad thing. For example, portions
priced per pound of spinach or beet scoadalia, tar-
ragon potato salad and pasta with black olives all
give you a pretty decent bang for your buck. They
serve lentil and chicken noodle soup daily ($1.99).
And next to the soup you can find muska borek
(60¢) which is absolutely delicious (hot spinach
and feta cheese in phyllo dough), but is almost
always sold out by the time we get there. So get
there early and often!

Pakistani and Trinidadian United Nation Halal Food

Fish, Pakistani, Street-cart, Trinidadian

**North side of 43rd Street (east of Sixth Avenue)
Monday – Friday, 11 a.m. – 5 p.m.**

Post 9/11, this immensely popular street cart changed its name from Healthy Halal to Pakistani and Trinidadian United Nation Halal Food. The name's unwieldy, but pretty darn descriptive. We asked the co-owner of the stand how such an unusual amalgam came about and she told us that her husband is from Pakistan and she's from Trinidad. Duh! Hundreds of hungry lunchers descend daily upon P.A.T.U.N.H.F. (you think we're typing that name again?) to feast on their mega-cheap, ultra-tasty selections.

Pakistan's influence is felt most directly in the all-consuming smell of curry that permeates the area and taunts you as you drool in line. The chicken is the best of their curries and is drenched in the pungent yellow sauce as it simmers. Served over long grained white or mellow basmati rice, the curry chicken comes in a small but filling portion ($3.50) or a gut-busting larger one ($4.50). Wonderful greens and potatoes are free, so have them ladle on the veggies. A soothing white sauce and a buzzingly persistent hot sauce are available and delicious in tandem.

Jet over to Trinidad if you're in the mood for fish. The superb fried whiting is coated in a tantalizing mixture of spices and herbs and deep-fried before your eyes. The frying is fast but not instant, so let them know you want fish before getting in line; it'll be ready for you when you get to the front. The fish goes on top of rice and is covered with a mixture of chickpeas, cabbage, broccoli and onions. The small portion ($4) is plenty for all but the ravenous. The dish is absolutely fantastic and not a bit fishy or greasy.

P.A.T.U.N.H.F. is the Henry Ford of street-carts, having perfected the art of the street-cart assembly line. It's poetry in curry as four venders work in perfect harmony to speedily knock out orders. Grace Pavilion is directly across 43rd street and Bryant Park is just one block south, so there's plenty of seating options nearby.

Pizza Villagio

Italian, Pizza

153 W. 57th St. (bet. Sixth and Seventh avenues)
Seven days, 9:30 a.m. – 11 p.m.
(212) 957-9580
(212) 957-9581

Right across from Carnegie Hall, in theme restaurant central, Pizza Villagio is a welcome refuge from places where you pay $20 for the privilege of eating lunch near Bob Marley's suspenders or Schwarzenegger sweatband.

Tax is included in all the prices on the wall, so leave your calculator at home. The pizza slices ($2 and up) are zesty with plenty of gooey cheese and particularly good pepperoni. The chicken roll ($3.60) is not a bit dry, and is delicious dunked donut-style in a cup of hot marinara. Breaded mozzarella sticks (3 for a dollar) are very tempting, but the garlic knots are far better.

For five bucks straight up, you can stuff yourself on a manicotti or ravioli platter, each of which comes with a serving of rice or spaghetti and a roll. Starch, anyone? The manicotti platter nestles three large ricotta filled tubes on top of a plateful of spaghetti with a very pleasant slightly sweet marinara.

Villagio's salad selection is varied, inexpensive and delicious. Displayed behind glass downstream from the pizza counter, tuna pasta salad, chicken pasta salad, gardiniera salad and Greek salad are a few of their tempting choices. All the small salads are $3.45 and they often throw in a bonus, like a stuffed grape leaf balanced on top of the Greek.

In the attractive brick-adorned seating area, there is a large water dispenser; so don't waste a Washington on a can of soda. They have seating for about 30 at small tables that many days are covered with red tablecloths and white doilies straight out of that spaghetti-kissing scene from *Lady & the Tramp*.

Pluck U.

Wings

768 Ninth Ave. (bet. 51th and 52th streets)
Monday – Friday, 11 a.m. – 10 p.m.
Saturday, 12 p.m. – 10 p.m.
Sunday, 1 p.m. – 10 p.m.
(212) 582-2468
www.pluckuny.com

Started by two college buddies (hmmm, sounds a little like this book), Pluck U. is actually not named for its implied expletive, but rather for Pluck University, an accredited center for fowl learning. And this one room school house has blossomed into four locations in Manhattan, none better than the midtown establishment. With its young staff, kitschy high-chair tables and mounted blaring TV's, all you need is a pitcher of beer to feel like you just walked into your favorite college hangout.

Gracing the south wall of Pluck U. is the Sauce-O-Meter. We call it the Wailing Wall; it's here you decide how spicy you want your wings. You can opt for the sweet BBQ flavor, go for death (the hottest sauce they serve) or chose from three varying degrees in-between. While we think the sauces aren't as spicy as described, be careful with Death, since it's the "Suicide, Chernobyl, 3 Mile Island" sauce. The BBQ is correctly labeled "For the WIMPS," but is cool and tangy. To mix things up a little, you can try the Gold sauce, a slightly spicy blend of molasses, mustard, apple cider vinegar, cayenne and other spices.

For $4.60, the #1 combo comes with 5 wings, small fries and a regular fountain soda. The wings are solid, with a flavorful sauce, and with only 5 wings to the order, it's a good thing they're quite meaty. The small fry is much larger than expected, and rather good. Served in a paper cup (like all good fries are), they are salty enough to satisfy the taste buds, without over doing it. And if you like fries with the skins left on, these will definitely be to your liking. And what would a wings meal be without a side of celery sticks with blue cheese dipping sauce? They're thrown in with each combo meal.

Pluck U. does have a varied menu in addition to the wings, like its grilled chicken sandwich ($3.65). Served on a seeded hamburger bun, topped with fresh lettuce, tomatoes, onions and mayo, the grilled chicken sandwich is made even better when garnished with the tasty BBQ sauce. And if you come to town with 39 of your favorite friends, you've got to indulge in party platter #2, 200 wings, four buckets of fries and 10 pounds of cole slaw. Including tax, all this can be yours for just $4.07 a person. Sorta makes you yearn for those college days.

Potato King

Baked Potatoes, Street-cart

South side of 50th Street
(between Sixth and Seventh avenues)
Monday – Friday, 11 a.m. – 5 p.m.

If you were in Ireland and craved a potato during the Great Potato Famine of 1845 you were probably out of luck. If you currently frequent midtown and have the same hankering, however, you're all set. While there are many who call themselves cheap food royalty, several of whom made this illustrious guide, none are as starchy as the Potato King. The cart of the friendly Potato King is stocked with huge spuds and, for $3.50, you can have one smothered with one of the many toppins. They've got the classics like butter and sour cream, as well as more filling alternatives like mixed-vegetable succotash, chili, salsa and beans and, of course, the ever popular broccoli and cheese. If you opt for melted cheese, be warned; it's the plasticy cheese-sauce you get on nachos at a ballgame.

Before King Carbo piles on the stuff, however, he pulls the old "split and smush," a technique where he splits the tater and crushes it (with gloved hands) from either end towards the middle, thusly breaking up the center and creating a nice bed for the toppings. The P. King benevolently provides shakers full of complimentary Bacon Bits for your personal potato pleasure. You can even substitute a sweet potato for 50¢ extra.

(continued)

As well as being a great vegetarian draw, the spud sovereign is one of the more popular streetcarts for health conscious lunchers. We're not sure, however, when a massive carbohydrate bomb of a potato drenched with butter and melted cheese was classified as "health food". C'mon, this place is Dr. Atkins's nightmare, the high temple of carbohydrates! But who are we to judge?

"Here's to the ladies who lunch. Aren't they the best?"

STEPHEN SONDHEIM

Le Rendez-Vous Café

Middle Eastern, Pizza, Sandwiches

739 Eighth Ave. (bet. 46th and 47th streets)
Seven days, 7 a.m. – 2 a.m.
(212) 265-2233

Humus and pizza...together at last. This very clean counter-café serves Middle Eastern fare and pizza, so it naturally has a French name...say what?! We can cut them some slack, though, they do have tasty French pastries displayed behind the bakery counter, and they do serve French toast, after all.

If you like breakfast for lunch, they have all sorts of options such as spinach omelets à la Florentine and the aforementioned French toast with maple syrup and bananas (both $3.50). You lunchy lunch eaters, however, should go Middle Eastern with the hot crispy falafel sandwiches ($2.95). Or, for the same price, you can nosh some 'noush, babaganoush, that is. Frankly, we like saying babaganoush so much, we'd pay more than they actually charge for it just so we could babble the word over and over. Babaganoush, babaganoush, babaganoush. Best deal: combo sandwich with falafel plus a choice of tabouli, hummus or babaganoush (isn't that fun?) for $3.50.

Their pizza counter has always been strong, and it seems to have improved. They've got their groove on and always seem to have just pulled bubbling pies right out of the cool looking brick oven.

95

Cheese slices are $1.85, a slice of Sicilian is $2 and it goes up from there.

The café has done some remodeling recently, and alas, has packed away most of their *I Dream of Jeannie*-style knick-knacks. What has not gone away, however, is the attentive service and clean atmosphere. Here's a cool option for family savings. With a purchase of $10 or more, they'll toss you a free 2 liter bottle of Pepsi: a laudable plan for which we give them a little round of applause that you, regretfully, can neither see nor hear. Perhaps you'll do it yourself, however, after you lunch there.

Seafood Street-cart

Fish, Korean, Sandwiches, Street-cart
South side of 46th Street (east of Sixth Avenue)
Monday – Friday, 11:30 a.m. – 4:30 p.m.

This unnamed street-cart is the anti-Moshe's plain and simple. Moshe's, of course, is the ultra-kosher falafel stand directly west of this place. While four bearded men fry up chickpea balls at Moshe's, one short Korean woman stands on a box and fries up shrimp and fish at her rolling seafood shack. The only thing they have in common is a vendetta against the American Heart Association and a great selection of affordable lunches.

You can't miss with any of the seafood sandwiches. Ask before you set your heart on a menu item, however, since seafood selections go in and out of season. Whiting ($3), flounder ($3.50) and shrimp sandwiches ($3) are usually available. The shrimp sandwich on a thick piece of grilled pita is excellent. Think gyro and add plenty of jumbo crispy shrimp to the daydream and you'll be close to the experience. For the flounder, she recommends a grilled French roll. The flounder is hot, quite tender on the inside and well accented by her white sauce (not tartar). We've got to underscore that she fries the fish to order. While that may mean a slightly longer wait, it also means that the fish is hot and not a bit fishy or greasy.

She serves other street-cart standbys like chicken heroes, beefsteak and chicken curry, but go for her native dishes and you'll be happy. The Korean-style tofu with bean curd and rice is $3 for a small and $4 for a regular. While the tofu is nice, the Korean-style barbequed short-ribs with rice and salad ($3.50 small / $5 large) is generously portioned and, to borrow a phrase, finger licking good.

"I never drink coffee at lunch.
I find it keeps me awake for the afternoon."

RONALD REAGAN

Tad's Steaks

Steaks

701 Seventh Ave. (bet. 47th and 48th streets)
Monday – Friday, 11 a.m. – 5 p.m.
(212) 768-0946

Ah, the great New York City steakhouses: Peter Luger's, The Palm, Sparks…Tad's? Alas, for a meat-and-potatoes type of guy, the pickings are few and far between for a $5 meal. You can't actually get a <u>steak</u> at Tad's Steaks for less than $5, though if you're craving a T-bone and want to splurge you can get one with trimmings for less than $10.

However, for $4.29 plus tax, between 11 a.m. and 4 p.m., you get the "ground beefsteak" daily lunch special: a chopped beefsteak, choice of potato, cole slaw and a piece of garlic bread. Sure it looks like a burger sans bun, but it delivers a rich sirloin taste a cut above "burger." The baked potato is…oh c'mon now; you can't screw up a baked potato. The huge slice of garlic toast is saturated with delicious garlic butter and complements a small portion of zippy coleslaw. The topper (literally) is the melted garlic butter ladled over the whole shebang. Your heart will beat out a frantic SOS, but the alarm is worth it.

No matter which Tad's you venture into (and there are seemingly as many Tad's in Times Square as there are scalpers with extra Phantom tickets), don't be scared off by the dingy cheap wood paneling or the sparse lighting. There is free water in groovy red plastic tumblers and busboys clearing away dirty dishes to the beat of piped-in Latin muzak. There's also a quarter-chicken lunch deal that fits the bill, but why eat chicken in a steakhouse? Garlic butter just goes better with beef.

"Time is an illusion. Lunchtime doubly so."

DOUGLAS ADAMS

Tony Sushi King/Pick a Bagel

Bakery, Sandwiches, Sushi

200 W. 57th St. (SW corner of Seventh Avenue)
Seven days, 5:30 a.m. – 12 a.m.
(212) 957-5151

This unlikely combination boasts a quality sushi counter linked to a high-end bagel/catering deli where your sushi-hating friend can get him or herself some occidental chow. It's what's called co-marketing, allowing both stores to split some costs.

Tony Sushi King (only in America), a side annex to Pick a Bagel, serves fresh sushi and rolls a notch above Daiichi or Teriyaki Boy. Their generous servings of steamy miso soup make an inexpensive satisfying meal possible in a cuisine notorious for leaving Americans wanting more. For just $1.50, you get the "small" miso soup (16 ounces!) which is flavorful with firm cubes of tofu floating among the slightly crunchy seaweed leaves. Accessorize the miso with a hand wrapped crunchy cucumber roll (8 cut pieces) for only $3. In a cone of seaweed paper, they artfully pile delicate slivers of cucumber into a scrumptious sculpture you'd expect to pay double for.

Want sushi when you eat sushi? Clam, shrimp or crab pieces are $1.50; mackerel, squid, octopus, caviar or salmon $1.80; tuna $2; eel $2.50; salmon roe $2.75; and yellow tail $2.80. Ninja-sword and paper lantern décor is entertainingly at odds with piped-in top 40 music.

Pick a Bagel's items compliment the sushi selection by providing amazing variety in this one establishment. Egg salad, flaky baked knishes and what seem to be about a thousand different salads and spreads are all available. The bagels are plump, quite good and come in a variety of flavors, so get your sandwich on one. A BLT on an onion bagel ($3.95) is tasty and filling, and if you want crispy bacon, you'd better ask.

There is lots of seating, but it's usually very crowded. If you're with a friend, one of you should stand in line while the other scouts for a table; it's never too early to put your quarter up on the machine.

Two Boots

Pizza

30 Rockefeller Center (Lower Dining Concourse)
Monday - Thursday, 11 a.m. – 8 p.m.
Friday, 11 a.m. – 7 p.m.
Saturday, 11 a.m. – 6 p.m.
(212) 332-8800

Two Boots is one of the most distinctive pizzerias in New York City. Their logo and name tell the whole story. Pull out an atlas and follow along. Italy (shaped like a boot) + Louisiana (shaped like a boot) = Two Boots. Cajun style pizza. Brilliant!

They've Cajun-ized two key pizza elements: the crust and the sauce. Most of their pies feature a remarkable corn-meal crust that is light and crackery yet strong enough not to sag or buckle. Each bite gives way with a satisfying crunch, and damn, the sauce is zippy! Plenty of jalapeños and garlic. Don't be afraid, it's not ridiculously hot, just ridiculously good; it delivers a nice buzz to your lips that in no way overpowers the taste of the slice. Try two slices of the regular cheese pie for the perfect introduction to Two Boots. At $2.15 per, it's more expensive than a Ray Bari slice, but Mardi Gras is worth the price of admission.

The heart of the menu is the selection of 12 specialty pies available by the slice for $3.50 per. The bayou beast piles on BBQ shrimp, crawfish, Andouille sausage and jalapeños and then chemically activates them with that spicy red sauce. Mrs. Peel is a vegetarian must-eat: a round Sicilian pie with roasted vegetables (including artichokes), fresh garlic and breadcrumbs. There's the night tripper: sun-dried tomatoes, roasted garlic and jalapeño pesto on a white pie with a spinach crust. Or Tony Clifton: wild mushrooms, vidalia onions and sweet red pepper pesto. Beyond the 12, they even serve a special pie of the day sans the snappy name. For example, the anonymous but outstanding pie with marinated chicken, Calabria sauce and cilantro.

For our shut-in readers, you can get a piece of Mel Cooley, Mr. Pink, Cleopatra Jones or Tony Clifton online. Those are names of specialty slices, by the way, and we are talking about pizza delivery. If you're in their delivery area, click your way over to www.homedelivery.com ($10 minimum for delivery). Coming soon, a new location in the 1 Times Square building.

Universal Café

Burgers, Sandwiches

977 Eighth Ave. (bet. 57th and 58th streets)
Seven days, 5 a.m. – 11:30 p.m.
(212) 262-2561

Borrowing from the bookstore trend, Universal News, the New York magazine shop, has added a café to its store. And why not? Reading a UFO magazine is all the more exciting while sipping on a café mocha and eating a pumpkin tea cake.

The main reason to lunch at Universal Café is to relax and peruse its gargantuan stock of over 7,000 international and domestic magazines while you munch. The hundreds of magazine categories include cigar, yachting, hair, knitting/crochet, teen, aviation, and Africa. As you wait for your food, chose a 'zine, find a table and prepare to dine quietly, surrounded by readers, relaxers and workers, all free to stay as long as they like.

Universal Café is one of the few bookstores with a large and varied lunch selection. Start with the spotless salad bar, where you can create your own meal from a selection of vegetables, pastas and bean salads. Or go the sandwich route. Served on your choice of 8 different breads, including focaccia and pita, you can come away with a delicious deal like the tuna salad ($4.25) with tomato, avocado and sprouts.

There's always the pasta salad of the day ($3.25 small / $4.50 large); if you like parsley, the orzo

---

salad is a must, featuring yellow zucchini and carrots. Or try the Cajun turkey burger ($4) smothered in a thick barbeque sauce. It tastes more like meatloaf than turkey, with spicy bits of roasted peppers commanding much of the flavor. (Make sure the helpful staff heats the burger up properly, as they're quite thick and have a tendency to come out cold in the middle.)

Enjoy your lunchtime read. Just try not to get barbeque sauce on that European Models Quarterly before you reshelve it.

Wrapsody

Hot Dogs/Sausages

692 Eighth Ave. (bet. 43rd and 44th streets)
Seven days, 8 a.m. – 9 p.m.
(212) 221-9280

While it's no surprise that conventional wraps like the taste of honey wrap (fancy chicken salad) monopolize the menu, it's the low fat chicken sausages that set Wrapsody apart from its competitors. This unusual lunch is, as the menu proclaims, "music to your mouth" and turns an ordinary sandwich shop into a Bohemian rhapsody.

There are three low-fat chicken sausages from which to choose: ginger, shiitake mushroom and cilantro; sun-dried tomatoes and mozzarella; and chipolte pepper. Each sausage comes smothered in one of these free toppings: barbecued onions, pineapple salsa, black bean, onions and peppers or sweet onions. It's a daunting task choosing a perfect sausage-topping combination because the toppings are much more than an afterthought; their bold flavors don't just complement, they collaborate with the delectable sausages. These low-fat sausages are grilled along side your choice of wrap or roll, adding to the back-yard flavor. The sausages are hearty as well as heart-smart, and you can complement them with a refreshing piece of fruit for a quarter.

Aside from the sausages, Wrapsody has six health smoothies made with non-fat frozen yogurt, vanilla soy milk or apple or orange juice. They feature daily healthy soup alternatives like gazpacho or lentil with spinach. There are fresh salads too, like a spinach salad with honey Dijon dressing for only $3.95. They even stock a wide selection of Fresh Samantha fruit juices. The sheer quantity of reasonably priced ultra-healthy options is quite impressive.

But it was only a matter of time before this health conscious rebel turned to the dark side. Their latest addition? Belgian fries. So pick your poison.

Yip's Pow Wok

Chinese

129 W. 48th St. (bet. Sixth and Seventh avenues)
Monday – Friday, 11 a.m. – 5 p.m.
(212) 391-2742

Formerly just Yip's, this midtown budget favorite has very filling portions of delicious Chinese food and an airy contemporary atmosphere. The lines are always long but move lightning fast and they end at a spotless glass-paned counter where you can see your food before ordering ("Uh, what's that one? What about that one?"). The service is friendly and helpful, the chalk-wall menu has plenty of variety and the prices include tax. Incredibly, sixteen of the lunch specials are less than $5. A special includes several large ladles-full of your entrée over an extremely generous portion of white rice, brown rice or lo mein. Dishes are served in sturdy plastic containers with snap-on tops perfect for take-out that the truly thrifty will want to save for future kitchen use.

The food is hot, fresh and delicious. Beef and broccoli, the litmus test of any Chinese place, passes with flying colors: full of generous slices of beef in a delectable brown sauce. Their orange chicken is mandatory, the sesame chicken is tantalizing and the spicy pepper chicken is wonderfully zesty and... um...peppery ($4.95 each). Other options include chicken with eggplant, mixed veggies with garlic sauce and, of course, General Tso's chicken.

109

(continued)

It's very tough to find a table right away, but by the time you get some chopsticks, duck sauce and free water (dispensed from large coolers) something should free-up.

What more could you want? A second location? You got it! Although the space is a little cramped and the décor isn't as fashionable, this mini-Yip's located at 52 W. 52nd St. boasts the same great food and service. Yip, yip, hooray!

"Miss Otis regrets she's unable to lunch today."

COLE PORTER

Yoshinoya

Japanese

255 West 42nd St.
 (between Seventh and Eighth avenues)
Monday – Friday, 10 a.m. – 3 a.m.
(212) 703-9940

Almost across the street from the strange theater-like McDonald's on 42nd Street is the McDonalds of Japanese fast food. You may not have heard of Yoshinoya and they may not have served "billions and billions", but the Times Square location is their thousandth store and it puts out bowl after bowl of tasty inexpensive grub.

A regular sized beef or teriyaki chicken bowl ($3.59) is a good-sized bowl of rice topped by a generous heap of your meat choice in a savory sauce. Simple, affordable and hearty, this is an ideal on-the-go meal. Vegetable bowls are available for $2.99.

The chicken salad ($4.19) is plenty hefty for a hungry luncher. Plenty of chicken, plenty of greens and several dressings to choose from. It's topped off with those crunchy Asian noodles too.

Get this. You can get the chicken entrées "skinless". How cool is that? Also, a sign states that they serve "raw eggs – dine-in only". We have no idea what that means. Are they afraid of teen hoodlums egging cars? We really don't know.

To round out your meal, a small fountain drink runs $1.09 and a piece of cheesecake or caramel flan costs $1.59. They make a light flavorful miso soup ($1.29) full of protein packed tofu.

The look is modern Asian, if glass hanging lamps in primary colors are modern and if faux bamboo trees are Asian, that is. Shakers full of hot red pepper flakes, bottles of soy sauce and bins of shredded pickled cabbage are available at the condiment counter. Seating for approximately 40.

Z-Deli

Sandwiches

803 Eighth Ave. (bet. 48th and 49th streets)
Seven days, 24 hours
(212) 315-1659

Most places that try to do it all usually do it all poorly. Z-Deli seems to do it all splendidly from A to... well, from A to Z. Z-Deli is a crowded but organized storefront on Eighth Avenue between 48th and 49th streets where they have catering, a deli-counter and convenience store shelves. For our purposes, their deli-counter (b'fast, lunch and dinner) is the issue at hand. On any given day, they literally have 30 to 40 sandwiches for less than $5 dollars including a can of soda. Many of these you can get on a hero (40¢ extra) and still get out for less than $5: unbelievable. It gets even better, race fans. The can-o'-soda selection is remarkable. In addition to the usual suspects like Coke, Pepsi, 7-Up and Sprite, they have all the cool seldom seen cans like Fanta and Ch-ch-ch-cherry Coke (outrageous)!

Back to the sandwiches. They of course have all the basics like turkey, roast beef, BLT and pastrami (ranging from $3-$4), but we heartily recommend one of their myriad of ridiculously named sand-wiches which, for the most part, in grand deli tra-dition, have very little to do with the contents of the sandwich. The Times Square, for example, has "red" corned beef, melted Swiss cheese, lettuce and onion: delicious. That on a hero with a cold

113

can of Cherry Coke runs a paltry $4.60. No worries here, tax is included in all the prices. Since they do the catering thing, there's a million different salads and concoctions on hand with which to make wacky sandwiches: curry chicken, Caesar salad, Dijon chicken, New Orleans red chicken and honey curry chicken, to name a few.

Wanna hear our theory? Their secret is that they make their different businesses work with one another rather than against. The catering business naturally provides variety to their lunch and dinner menu and perhaps their typically overpriced convenience store shelves help to keep the deli prices low for their grateful customers. There's no seating so take the take-out to nearby World Wide Plaza if the weather's nice.

5 EXCEPTIONAL PLACES FOR "A LITTLE MORE"

For the following five reviews, pretend the title of this guide is *The $7 Lunch*. They were just so good, we couldn't bear not including them. They meet all the criteria for this guide except that their entry-level prices are a bit more than five bucks. So if you have a couple extra Sacagaweas or Suzy B.'s from the Metrocard machine burning a hole in your pocket, check these out.

"Manhattan is a narrow island off the coast of New Jersey devoted to the pursuit of lunch."

RAYMOND SOKOLOV

Diamond Dairy of New York Restaurant

Kosher, Sandwiches

4 W. 47th St., Mezzanine
  (between Fifth and Sixth avenues)
Monday – Thursday, 7:30 a.m. – 5:30 p.m.
Friday, 7:30 a.m. – 2 p.m.
(212) 719-2694

Diamond Dairy is truly a hidden gem. If you peer through the front windows of the International Diamond Exchange on Diamond Row, you'll see a staircase way in the back left that leads to an eating experience you could only have in New York. Up on the mezzanine is a glatt kosher dairy restaurant catering mostly to diamond industry merchants and workers. Sitting at the counter or at a rickety table overlooking the busy diamond market, Hassidic Jews down slishkele and cholent while making deals on cell phones. Harried waitresses bustle here and there explaining "No sardines today, some kreplach maybe?"

We've gotta say upfront that their tuna sandwich ($3.50) is one of the best in Manhattan. That said, they've got the whole shmear: eggs and omelettes, salads, soups, fish, sandwiches, specials and desserts.

The excellent borscht ($2.95) is served cold with sour cream (everything's served with sour cream). Don't let the color scare you. Beets are simply the sweetest member of the potato family. The potato pancakes ($4.50 small / $6 large) are way better

117

than Katz's. The time from frying pan to your mouth is measured in seconds, which means crispy, crispy, crispy. At $3.50, the vegetarian chopped liver sandwich is a real treat and much lighter than its fleishig (meat) cousin. The cold marinated salmon ($8.50) is very nice with a surprisingly sweet marinade and comes with hot or cold vegetables. The pirogies ($4.50 small / $6.45 large) are enormous and served boiled or fried. These are old-school delicious and filled with smooth potato, but sorry, no bacon bits in the filling here. For dessert, potato or rice pudding is $2 and required eating.

Diamond Dairy doesn't stop at the expected. It tries its glatt kosher hands at linguini, lo mein, chow mein and goulash as well. Just try not to giggle if you order "fish balls and spaghetti" ($6.75).

Pay the cashier, who'll guilt your change into the enormous row of pushkies (charity boxes) displayed in front of the register with a practiced head tilt and glance downward. Plunking your change is the perfect way to alleviate the complimentary serving of guilt which comes with everything on the menu and goes well with sour cream or applesauce.

Go Sushi

Japanese, Sushi

756 Ninth Ave. (SE corner of 51st Street)
Seven days, 11:30 a.m. – 11:30 p.m.
(212) 459-2288
(212) 459-3379

Someone finally figured out that between $40 a person sushi restaurants and ultra-chewy pre-packaged sushi lies an enormous opportunity. There is a huge market of sushi-lovers on a budget who would love to eat Japanese food several times a week if they could afford it. Now they can. Go Sushi crunched the numbers somehow to bring us high quality fast-food Japanese.

They do have a refrigerated shelf at the counter with pre-packaged sides and sushi rolls such as seaweed salad ($2.50), edamame ($3.50) and inside-out California rolls ($3.80). Behind the counter, however, the enormous staff makes most of the sushi and entrées fresh. Sushi pieces à la carte are extremely well priced; none of their 14 offerings are more than $2 per. You won't find the very high end items here such as giant clam or fatty tuna, but most of the usual suspects are in the line-up. Most importantly, the fish is very fresh, generously cut and well presented.

The best deals are the combos. The Go Sushi box ($5.95) includes one piece each of tuna and salmon sushi, four pieces of California roll, soba noodles and a mixed green salad with tasty ginger dressing. The sushi regular deal ($6.95) includes two salmons, one tuna, one shrimp and four pieces each of salmon and California roll. Sashimi meals include miso soup and rice or salad but are pricier ($9.95-$16.95).

For a more filling meal go for one of the attractive bento boxes: a lacquered wooden box with separate compartments for each portion of your meal. The excellent beef negimaki box ($5.95) features thin slices of beef rolled around scallion centers in a savory brown sauce. Two delicate steamed shrimp dumplings, white or brown rice and a mixed green salad complete this aesthetic and gastronomic treat.

The atmosphere is cafeteria chic: simple and non-pretentious with neat rows of tables and a gleaming metallic magazine rack at one end of the dining area. For dessert you've gotta try the red bean cake ($1.75). Ubiquitous in Japan, these rice and red bean doughnuts are the Snickers of the Pacific Rim.

Kinokuniya Bookstore Café

Japanese, Sandwiches

10 W. 49th St. (bet. Fifth and Sixth avenues)
Seven days, 11 a.m. – 7 p.m.
First Friday of every month, no sandwiches available, traditional cakes served
(212) 765-7766
www.kinokuniya.com

The tea counter at the center of Kinokuniya Bookstore is an island of calm near the middle of Rockefeller Center, one of the most hectic tourist areas in Manhattan. The speckled blue counter with black trim is ringed by black swivel chairs that probably looked futuristic around 1979. This funkiness is surrounded in turn by counters and rows and stacks of books that, to a non-Japanese reader, are more art than text. This lack of English contributes to the serenity; no buzz-words or headlines grabbing your attention, just beautiful illustrations and graceful Japanese kanji by the millions. Just to remind you that you're not in Tokyo, however, two huge television sets are inset in the wall above the counter and are usually tuned to local cable station New York 1 (with the sound turned way down).

Our recommendation for lunch is the sandwich and tea combination ($7). The tea, as you'd expect, is made with art and precision. Your choice of three loose teas – Assam, Earl Grey, Golden Kenya – is packed into the bottom of a French press. After the server pours boiling water onto the tea from about three feet above, it is allowed to steep. The Assam is the best choice if you like milk in your tea while lemon-lovers would do well with Golden Kenya. Ironically, the Japanese tea-sandwiches are served on china and are a gastronomic study in geometry. At first glance, you've been served a rectangular block of bread and fillings. Upon closer examination, however, the block separates into four dainty sandwiches: tuna, ham, egg salad and tomato with cucumber. Each sandwich is perfectly crustless and measures about five by three inches and maybe one half inch thick. Each, without being the slightest bit bland, is milder than the next. Filling, but not overly so, the sandwich and tea lunch is transcendental meditation for your mouth.

À la carte, coffee (brewed fresh one cup at a time) is $1.50, tea is $3 ($2.50 from 11 a.m. till noon), the sandwich set runs $4.50 and a piece of cake is $3.50. They do tend to run out of sandwiches early, so don't dawdle.

Luigi's

Italian, Pizza, Sandwiches, Soup/Salad

910 Eighth Ave. (NE corner of 54th Street)
Seven days, 11 a.m. – 11 p.m.
(212) 245-8432

If Luigi of Nintendo fame had gone into the restaurant biz instead of plumbing with his cousin Mario, maybe he wouldn't need to run around all day with those monsters and mutated turtles.

Luigi's, a family Italian restaurant and pizzeria, is one of those rare Manhattan havens that bring everybody together. On any given day, you're likely to lunch next to a celebrity, or a policeman, or a suit, or Bowser, or an octogenarian couple or a bunch of actors on their lunch break. They're all at Luigi's for the same thing: mouth-watering heroes, tantalizing salads and great pizza and pasta.

It usually takes just one bite of the chicken Parmigiana hero ($6.25) to turn a first-time customer into a lifelong fan. Think warm breaded chicken topped with melted cheese, spiced with a marinara sauce the way Tony Soprano would like it and gift-wrapped in a perfectly toasted hero roll. It doesn't get much better than that.

But a little bit maybe. The chicken salad, perhaps Luigi's most popular item, is flat-out delicious. It'll put you back $7.50 for a large, but you'll get an enormous bed of lettuce topped generously with chunks of breaded chicken, large slices of juicy tomatoes and a couple of jumbo Mediterranean olives. The whole thing is doused in a vinaigrette dressing that makes you pucker with joy. And every salad comes with a side of Italian sesame-seeded bread, perfect for sopping up extra dressing.

Of course, they serve pasta and pizza too. The ziti with broccoli is served artfully in a fragrant garlic and oil sauce. And although Luigi's appears in this bonus section, the excellent and affordable pizza slices alone would have qualified it for the main part of this guide.

Don't be shy; with so many customers, it's easy to be left clamoring for the attention of someone behind the counter. While we're not officially condoning pushing or shoving, a glare and a hip check may be in order.

Yum Thai Cuisine

Thai

129 W. 44th St.
  (between Sixth Avenue and Broadway)
Monday – Friday, 11 a.m. – 9 p.m.
Saturday, 12 p.m. – 10 p.m.
(212) 819-0554

Yum earns the award for the most aptly named restaurant in Manhattan. If it didn't live up to its billing, would we be telling you about it?

At this Thai restaurant, it's hard to go wrong. But let us steer you in the general direction of number 42 on the menu, duck red curry, which is as flavorful as it is colorful. Green basil leaves, red chili peppers and tomatoes, yellow pineapple and brown duck are tossed in a milky curry sauce and crown a heap of white steamed rice. The duck is deliciously fatty, and the sweet pineapple cuts the biting kick of the curry, which is tinged with juicy coconut. This mélange of flavors is a real treat, and easily worth its $6.95 price tag.

Yum's pad thai ($6.50 for shrimp or chicken), the staple of any Thai establishment, is hearty and delicious. The rice noodles are cooked al dente, which seems just right. The bean sprouts are crispy, and the whole dish gets a notch better with a squeeze of the zesty lime on the side. If you find the chicken dry, don't despair; the side of spicy red chili sauce is the perfect solution. And can anyone tell us why tofu finds it way into all pad thai dishes in the universe? Is pad thai Thai for "Don't forget the soy cube."?

Yum has cozy seating for 20 along its walls which are colorfully adorned with the Thai alphabet. Free water dispensed at the front counter from a condensation-free jug is enigmatically cold. You will probably leave Yum stuffed (and sweaty from all the spicy food), but don't pass the candy bowl at the front counter without having a little dessert. Free sweets are all the sweeter.

PLACES TO TAKE
YOUR TAKEOUT

Many of the eateries in *The $5 Lunch* do not have seating. So here's a guide to 15 perfect places to take your take-out. Most of these are nice weather only; those marked with a ⌂, however, are indoors or covered.

Map on page 133

Places To Take Your Takeout

1. **BALSLEY PARK** – SE corner of 57th St. & Ninth Ave.

   Snapshot – The old flea market that used to occupy this area has been replaced by this green green green corner park where you can eat and then lay out for a tan.

   Tables / Chairs – Tables and chairs by Balsley Café plus benches and a sitting lawn.

2. **BRYANT PARK** – Sixth Avenue between 40th and 42nd streets

   Snapshot – Breathe easy in the tree-ringed backyard of the New York Public Library where relaxed mobs of lunchers carpet the lawn and circle the stone fountain.

   Tables / Chairs – Plenty of both, but hard to snag during lunch rush.

3. **CENTRAL PARK** – Begins on 59th Street (Central Park South) and runs north to 110th Street, from Central Park West to Fifth Avenue

   Snapshot – If you've got the time, pick a trail and get blissfully lost in the greatest urban park in the world. If you want to stay closer to midtown, however, here are a few prime lunching spots on the southern edge of the park:

   a. Merchant's Gate – southwestern corner of Central Park at 59th Street – beautiful sculpture group and benches

   b. Playground – directly north of the intersection of Seventh Avenue and Central Park South

   c. Hansom Cabs – Central Park South between Sixth and Seventh avenues – watch the horse and buggy drivers try to cheat tourists

d. The Pond – Go down the stairs on northeast corner of Central Park and Center Drive (Sixth Avenue) – benches line the walkway that winds around this peaceful pond

Tables / Chairs – Benches scattered throughout the park.

4. FISHER PARK – Connecting 54th and 55th streets just west of Sixth Avenue

Snapshot – Built in 1960, this tiny park borders the famous Ziegfeld movie theater and features towering fern as well as intriguing triangular hangings above a tranquil fountain.

Tables / Chairs – Tables and chairs for 28.

5 HOTEL PARKER MERIDIEN – 118 W. 57th St. Connecting 56th and 57th streets west of Sixth Avenue

Snapshot – A mirrored colonnade with a vaulted Byzantine ceiling leads to this comfortable lunch spot at the hotel where guests of the Rosie O'Donnell show stayed until she checked out.

Tables / Chairs – Two long rows of cushioned lobby chairs facing one another across a row of coffee tables.

Denotes indoor or covered seating

(continued)

Places To Take Your Takeout (continued)

6. **MMC PLAZA** – Connecting 45th and 46th streets between Fifth and Sixth avenues

   Snapshot – In this recently renovated plaza, the old swarms of pigeons have been replaced by a serene forest motif including fountains and an unlikely grove of five towering trees.

   Tables / Chairs – Many forest-green "woven" metal chairs bolted to the ground.

7. **THE NEW YORK PUBLIC LIBRARY TERRACE** – Fifth Avenue between 40th and 42nd streets

   Snapshot – Two immense stone lions guard you as you nosh and watch Fifth Avenue rush by.

   Tables / Chairs – Some of both to either side of the steps.

8. **PAINE WEBBER STONE TABLES** – North side of 51st Street just west of Sixth Avenue

   Snapshot – The smooth stone surfaces of these seats and tables are cool and coveted so you may need to wait for a vacancy.

   Tables / Chairs – Clusters of small inverted-cone-shaped stone tables surrounded by matching seats.

9. **REMI WALKTHRU** – Connecting 53rd and 54th streets between Fifth and Sixth avenues

   Snapshot – Glass brickwork and an impossibly high vaulted skylight define this space where you can always get a wide comfortable bench seat; if it's not too busy, Remi will usually look the other way and let you munch at one of their tables.

   Tables / Chairs – Plenty of bench seating plus "off-limits" Remi tables and chairs.

10 **ROCKEFELLER PLAZA CONCOURSE** – Under Rockefeller Plaza Pavilion (connecting 49th and 50th streets west of Fifth Avenue)

Snapshot – In good weather or bad, this ultra-clean area has a view of the rink, natural light and a $2 million glass sculpture. You could eat a $5 lunch every day for over a thousand years for that kind of dough and still be left with more than a quarter million dollars.

Tables / Chairs – Tables and chairs for 250.

11. **ROCKEFELLER PLAZA PAVILION** – Connecting 49th and 50th streets west of Fifth Avenue

Snapshot – This ravishingly beautiful national historic landmark has the famous rink surrounded by flags of the nations, the well-known Prometheus statue, immaculately manicured garden boxes and great international people watching.

Tables / Chairs – Lots of benches and chairs.

12. **SIXTH AVENUE STRIP** – The west side of Sixth Avenue from 48th to 52nd streets

Snapshot – Complementing this area's street-cart bonanza are the following pockets of seating:

a. outside 1211 Sixth Ave. – raised garden area with park benches

b. McGraw Hill building – raised garden area with park benches plus a downstairs area with green benches, a huge silver sculpture and frequent free concerts

c. outside 1251 Sixth Ave. – raised garden area with park benches plus an immense fountain with an edge perfect for sitting

Denotes indoor or covered seating

(continued)

d. northwest corner of Sixth Avenue and 50th Street – fountain with sit-friendly edge

e. northwest corner of Sixth Avenue and 51st Street – angled wooden benches plus a drinking fountain

f. southwest corner of Sixth Avenue and 52nd Street – stone monolithic benches sitting at skewed angles to one another

Tables/Chairs Various areas of benches and chairs.

13. UTSAV FOUNTAIN – Connecting 46th and 47th streets just west of Sixth Avenue

Snapshot – This breezeway outside the American Place Theatre and Utsav Indian Restaurant is anchored by an abstract sculpture fountain and flanked by shrub gardens.

Tables / Chairs – Plenty of seating surfaces.

14. PLAZA AT 888 SEVENTH AVE. – On the south side of 57th Street directly west of Brooklyn Diner

Snapshot – A row of huge metallic light posts faces a row of fourteen trees in this simple open air plaza.

Tables / Chairs – Plaza is lined on three sides with light green park seats.

15. WORLDWIDE PLAZA – Connecting 49th and 50th streets between Eighth and Ninth avenues

Snapshot – The old $3 movie theater here has closed, but the cheap spirit can be rekindled if you bring your $5 lunch for a feast in this enormous plaza.

Tables / Chairs – Plenty of seating, both chairs and fountain edges.

PLACES TO TAKE YOUR TAKEOUT

Central Park

"It is more fun to talk with someone who doesn't use long, difficult words but rather short, easy words like 'What about lunch?'"

POOH'S LITTLE INSTRUCTION BOOK,
POWERS AND SHEPARD

Index by Cuisine and Special Feature

Restaurants part of the "A Little More" section of the book

(continued)

Index by Cuisine and Special Feature (con't.)

Mexican
Burrito Box
The Border A La Carta
Fresco Tortillas

Middle Eastern
Halal Food
House of Pita
Lemon Tree Café
Moshe's
Le Rendez-Vous Café

Pakistani
Pakistani and Trinidadian
  United Nation Halal Food

Pizza
Associated Supermarket/
  Morton Williams Café
Cucina Gourmet
Famous Famiglia
Figaro Restaurant & Bar
Luigi's*
Pizza Villagio
Le Rendez-Vous Café
Two Boots

Popovers
New York Popover

Trinidadian
Pakistani and Trinidadian
  United Nation Halal Food

Sandwiches
Amy's Bread
Bagel Café
Balsley Café
D&S Marketplace
Daily Soup
Diamond Dairy of New York
  Restaurant*
Hello Deli
John's
Kinokuniya Bookstore Café*
Kwik Meal
Luigi's*
Margon Restaurant
Moshe's
New Era Café
New York Popover
Nick's
9th Avenue Cheese Market
Le Rendez-Vous Café
Seafood Street-cart
Tony Sushi King/
  Pick a Bagel
Universal Café
Z-Deli

Soup/Salad
Balsley Café
Bread Market Café
Daily Soup
Devon & Blakely
Hale and Hearty Soups
Luigi's*
New Era Café

Southern
Golden Chicken Ribs &
  Steak

THE $5 LUNCH

Steaks
Golden Chicken Ribs &
  Steak
John's
Tad's Steakhouse

Street-cart
The Border A La Carta
Cynthia & Robert
Halal Food
Hallo Berlin
Hot Dog King
John's
Kwik Meal
Moshe's
Nick's
Pakistani and Trinidadian
  United Nation Halal Food
Potato King
Seafood Street-cart

Sushi
Associated Supermarket/
  Morton Williams Café
Food Emporium
Go Sushi*
Tony Sushi King/
  Pick a Bagel

Thai
Yum Thai Cuisine*

Wings
Pluck U.

Restaurants part of the "A Little More" section of the book

Eddie's Top 5

❶ Moshe's

A sandwich the size of your head for $4? Oy! The
best falafel west (or east) of Tel Aviv.

❷ Fresco Tortillas

Incredible amounts of tasty Tex-Mex for your bucks.
Featuring delicious fresh-made tortillas and speed of
light service.

❸ Lemon Tree

Open till 11 p.m. for late night Middle Eastern
munchies. Great babaganoush and unparalleled
spinach pie.

❹ Margon

Impressive pressed Cuban sandwiches in a viva-
cious international atmosphere. The food and the
music insist you're in Miami; the Yankees and Mets
caps say otherwise.

❺ Tad's Steak

The pre-poured saran-wrapped glasses of wine are
so tacky, they're chic. Tad's changed my mantra to
"Everything's better with garlic butter."

Jeffrey's Top 5

❶ Moshe's

In 2000, Moshe's falafel made the "Top 10 Jewish Foods" in the nation, according to *USA Today*. I concur.

❷ Hallo Berlin

The wurst push-cart delivers German engineering done right. Forget the BMW – it's the Berliner with cabbage, potatoes and a roll for me.

❸ Amy's Bread

Delicate and delicious. Best bread in midtown combined with the freshest meats and the most flavorful condiments equals a sandwich to remember.

❹ Yip's Pow Wok

Lightening quick service, generous portions, great variety. Close your eyes, point randomly at a dish and you won't be disappointed.

❺ Pakistani & Trinidadian United Nation Halal Food

Curry drenched chicken and a zippy hot sauce combine for one hell of a lunch. Or delight in the fried fish. All this at a street-cart with the quickest service in New York.

www.thefivedollarlunch.com

Questions?

Comments?

E-mail us at:
info@thefivedollarlunch.com

The $5 Lunch Order Form

To purchase *The $5 Lunch* on-line, go to
www.thefivedollarlunch.com

Or

Send this form with a check or money order payable to:
  Sugarshu Books
  4555 Henry Hudson Parkway, #604
  Riverdale, NY 10471

Name: _____

Address: _____

City: _____

State: _____ Zip: _____

Telephone: _____

Email: _____

PLEASE SEND ME: _____

_____ books @ $12.95 . . . . . _____
(Quantity)

S&H @ $4.00 (per book)   . . . . . _____

                  TOTAL = _____

Please allow four weeks for delivery.

Notes

Notes

_____
_____
_____
_____
_____
_____
_____
_____
_____
_____
_____
_____
_____
_____
_____
_____
_____
_____
_____
_____
_____
_____
_____
_____
_____

www.thefivedollarlunch.com

Questions?

Comments?

E-mail us at:
info@thefivedollarlunch.com

SUGARSHU BOOKS • NEW YORK CITY, NEW YORK